THE CULTIVATED WILDERNESS

THE CULTIVATED WILDERNESS

OR, WHAT IS LANDSCAPE?

WITHDRAWN

PAUL SHEPHEARD

GRAHAM FOUNDATION FOR ADVANCED STUDIES IN THE
FINE ARTS
CHICAGO, ILLINOIS

THE MIT PRESS
CAMBRIDGE, MASSACHUSETTS
LONDON, ENGLAND

GF Publication of this book has been supported by a grant from the Graham Foundation for Advanced Studies in the Fine Arts.

This book was set in Melior by The MIT Press and was printed and bound in the United States of America.

Library of Congress Cataloging-in-Publication Data

Shepheard, Paul.
   The cultivated wilderness, or, What is landscape? / Paul Shepheard.
      p.   cm. — (Graham Foundation/MIT Press series in contemporary architectural discourse)
   ISBN 0-262-19380-9 (hardcover : alk. paper). — ISBN 0-262-69194-9 (pbk. : alk. paper)
      1. Landscape. I. Title. II. Series.
Arch BH301.L3S55   1997
   111'.85—dc20   96-31941
                                                                     CIP

CONTENTS

PREFACE

This book is about seeing things that are too big to see.

I have written about six landscapes, in an order of descending scale, and have given each landscape a thematic heading. The *Wilderness* of the book's title is the world before humans appeared in it, and the *Cultivation* is everything we've done to it since. *Landscape* is another name for the strategies that have governed what we've done.

Not so long ago I was teaching undergraduates in a school of architecture. It was a very argumentative time. One of the other teachers thought that Jim Dine's drawing of a coat hanger, the one rendered in soft graphite as though it were a study of the Venus de Milo, was sublime art. *The bringing of the ordinary into the realm of consciousness,* he called it. How I yelled at him! I thought he was corrupting youth with that sort of talk, so I yelled. You would have thought I was a baby in a carriage. The two of us sat there surrounded by bemused sophomores while he defended his narrative concoctions and I loudly berated his pretension.

"Every time I pick up a coat hanger I marvel at it," was what I shouted. "There is no ordinary in the world! No two things are the same!" I said that I thought he had been fooled by the machinery. "If you look hard enough," I insisted, "you will see that no two things are the same."

I came across him once with a bunch of students poring over photographs of men and women who were oiled and naked and penetrating each other with lighted candles. Is this the thing they call Art? He was using the images to generate a discussion about *spatial syntax.*

"Look, man," he said when I stopped to pour scorn on his project, "You're early Wittgenstein and I'm late Wittgenstein. That's the difference between us."

This prickly time led directly to my first book, *What Is Architecture?* published in 1994 by the MIT Press. It was my attempt to clarify the subject. I wanted to lever architecture out of the narrative crack my generation had wedged it into— wedged it so hard, indeed, that explanation had come to substitute for experience, the graphics were taken for the real thing, and grown people wondered aloud how virtual reality would change the environment.

Architecture is not just buildings, my argument goes. It is not everything, but it is more than buildings. No narrative can encompass it, no revelation can solve it. Action is required: architecture is the art of the solid, uncompromising, conclusive, material world. What we need in order to come to grips with its finality is not theories of *interpretation*—those narratives— or theories of *being*—those revelations—but theories of *action.*

The subject of cultivation and the wilderness, and what landscape is, first came clear to me at thirty thousand feet over the North Atlantic, en route from London to Boston. The man next to me was systematically drinking himself into oblivion, and we fell into conversation. He started it.

"Damn!" he said. "There goes another two thousand feet." We had changed altitude as we came into controlled airspace, and he was the only one of us passengers to notice it. It turned out he had flown transports for the air force in the early part of the jet age, and although he was a grandfather—he showed me pictures of a dozen cute kids—he just could not get used to being in a plane with someone else at the controls. The only way he could get through the experience was by sinking one glass of bourbon after another and listening for the sounds of the hydraulics cutting in and out.

I talked to him, to try and contain the fear he was radiating. I pointed down at the powder-blue ocean, smattered with clouds and lit up by that fabulous upper-atmosphere sunlight that's exclusive to air travel. "Is that not the most beautiful sight?" I said.

"God's earth," he said. "God's light." He woozily started to recite the first chapter of Genesis: "In the beginning God created the heaven and the earth." He shut his eyes while he was saying it—"And God said, Let there be light: and there was light"—opening his eyes again as he said the last word. "Damn! Auxiliary unit just cut in," he said, pointing his glass at a passing flight attendant. "How many pounds of fuel we got left, honey? Can you find out for me?"

Because he knew the book of Genesis so well, I got him to take me through the whole process of dividing night from day, heaven from earth, land from water, the sun from the stars. "Wait a minute," I said, "the sun and the moon came after night and day?"

"It's an allegory, for God's sake, listen: He brought forth the whales from the sea, the cattle from the land, the man from the beasts, and the woman from the man."

Whether Genesis is an allegory or the facts is an ancient question; nevertheless, the action of dividing one into two is how living things grow. Seeds and eggs have a genetic program called *exogenesis,* which destines them to be what they will be. Natural growth is not like the human action of cultivation, which may indeed be a process of division, or it may be the opposite, a synthesis; the difference is that, unlike natural growth, cultivation has no inevitability to it.

"That's what I said," he said: "It's an allegory of absoluteness."

So Adam and Eve and paradise are all part of the wilderness, is that it? And cultivation is an attempt to mend the world, broken as it was by the fall from grace? That's not how I see it. My friends call me a fundamentalist, but I do not yearn for paradise. This book is about the world we live in now.

I sat and watched the coast of Nova Scotia inching its way past the window, and my companion arrested another flight attendant and lifted another little bottle of bourbon from her tray. I asked him if sinking shots of Canadian Club to drown the fear of another man's flying was a common strategy among ex-pilots.

"Strategy? Did you say *strategy*? Hell, no, this is *operational!* This is front-line stuff! I'm drinking to stay alive, here!" Strategy is something done by generals, not pilots, he said. If the world knew what the difference between strategy and tactics was, he said, the world would be running on smooth rails.

"So what is it?" I asked him, just as the plane plunged into a pocket of turbulence. His eyes lit up like a kid on a roller coaster and he let out a little *whoop!* and raised his glass in the air—and then suddenly furrowed his brow and launched into a story about ancient Greece, and how clear and strong democracy was back then. He spoke like a man running out of time, laying a hand on my sleeve to make sure I paid attention. He described the debating chamber at Athens, half a millennium before Christ, way before the invention of any technology we take for granted now—but with a democracy so comprehensive it had no delegation. "Everyone could exercise his vote in person," he said. This is two white middle-class males talking, jetting across the Northern Hemisphere in a nitrous-oxide-spitting contaminator of the environment, so his use of the word *everyone* might need a little qualification—"Everyone who had a vote in Athens could exercise it in person," was what he meant. "No delegates. No members of Congress. No members of Parliament. Now then—once upon a time in Athens a question comes up," he said, warming to his story. "The Persians are about to invade us. Any ideas? Any suggestions for *action*? One man says 'Run!' Okay, that's one strategy. Another says 'Hide!' Okay—that's another. Then a third man gets on his feet and says 'Stand and fight!' That's his strategy for dealing with the invasion, to stand and fight; and they all start arguing and say to him, 'How are we, artists, farmers, slaveowners, going to fight?' And he says, 'We get long spears, organize ourselves into platoons, and attack them when they hit the beach. We fire and retire in turn.' They like the sound of it. They put the three strategies to the vote, and everyone votes to stand and fight."

He leaned back in his seat and looked at me like an actor surveying his audience. He seemed to single me out, even though I was the only one listening. "This man, he could be anyone, any citizen of Athens. It could be someone like you or someone like me. But he thought up the strategy, so he gets the job of general." This is the greatness of Athenian democracy: it was backed by personal commitment. "'Go ahead,' they say to him. 'It's your strategy, you lead us into battle. We're all behind you.'"

He looked at me as though he himself had been placed in this heroic driving seat, with dignity, strength, and compassion—when suddenly the expression slipped clean off his face.

"Damn! Mainwheel doors just opened," he said. "Can you hear the wheels coming down?" He shut his eyes and moved his lips as if counting, until a tiny distant clunk relieved him and he took another slug of bourbon to celebrate: "Okay! Wheels locked! Starting final approach!"

"We're not quite finished yet," I said. "If that's strategy, what's tactics? Sharpening the spears and arranging people into platoons and getting down to the beach?"

"That's it. And operations is getting down to the fighting itself," he said, all slow and inebriated again, raising his glass and bumping his nose against the ice cubes like a Russian submarine pushing its way out into the Baltic.

Whenever the cultivation of the wilderness comes up when I'm around, stories of religion and warfare start to migrate toward it. It's not because I'm devout or pugnacious; it's because these are subjects embroiled in the human struggle with the wilderness: how to explain it and how to own it. I would as soon have talked to this man about geology or natural history or cartography—the real investigation of the wilderness. I would as soon have talked about the way cultivation arises out of the circumstances people find themselves in, and out of the piece of globe they are inhabiting at the time. This is the stuff of the cultivation of the wilderness. It's what this book is about. But by now, the buffeting of a rough descent had plunged the whole plane into silent apprehension. My companion sat quiet, stupefied by alcohol, and I was left to my own little meditation on the subject of the landscape.

"You got strategy, the overview. You got tactics, the putting into position. You got operations, the carrying out," he had said as we passed over Massachusetts Bay. *That's fine,* I thought. *That's architecture.* There are buildings in the middle: tactics. There are the machines at the close end of the scale: operations. And there is landscape at the other. Landscape is the overview, the strategy.

When we disembarked in Boston my seatmate followed me, without overcoat or baggage, still clutching his bourbon glass, and so relieved to be back on the ground that he couldn't stop smiling—until we reached the checkout counter and they told him to get back on the plane. He was booked through to Philadelphia. He had to retrace his steps, get back into his seat, fasten his seatbelt, and endure another whole cycle of takeoff and landing. He stopped at the gate and looked back over his shoulder at me. He looked like a man on his way to the gallows.

———

What Is Architecture? is about landscapes, buildings, and machines. This book, *The Cultivated Wilderness,* is about those landscapes. I regard the chapter titles—"Unity," "Hope," "Nation," and so on—as first-stage strategies, and the descriptions of landscapes that follow each title are strategic positions—I would call them *themes,* because I want to reclaim the word from the world of Disney—and these themes give value to the first stage. The emphasis on strategies comes from those earlier thoughts about theories of action.

Every architectural move is set in a landscape strategy. The eighteenth-century grid cities of the New World are a strategy of reason, for example. Norman England was constructed as a network of strong points, in a strategy of occupation. Our predominant landscape strategy now is the economic exploitation of the earth. Rents, farming, industrial development, infrastructure—this strategy is an amorphous thing, expressed in a series of coincidental collisions, in which we are simultaneously rewarded and deprived. But covered up by this blanket of commerce are a multitude of other strategies, many other ways to treat the surface of the earth, some of which I have endeavored to reveal in this book.

When I started this project, I thought it was going to be called *The Seven Lamps of Landscape,* in homage to John Ruskin. The key words he titles his essays with sound a bit like mine, but they are more like the pieces of the armor of God that St. Paul describes in his letter to the Ephesians. I realize now that Ruskin's subject in *The Seven Lamps of Architecture* is a series of meditations on one theme—that *buildings are made in the sight of God*—and not strategies in themselves.

When I was about halfway through, I became aware that I was attempting to write about everything—all the cultivation that has ever been done, the whole human effort in reshaping the world. What I realize now is that although everywhere the world is the same as itself, landscape is nowhere the same as itself: you have to show landscape by example, because as a subject it won't reduce to fundamentals; it won't *trivialize.* Landscape as horticulture will; landscape architecture will—but that's tactics. Strategies are unique to themselves.

This exemplary quality means that my list of chapter titles could never be complete. I could add "Experiment," for example, and use Cape Hatteras as a theme: the spit of sand dunes in North Carolina where the Wright brothers experimented with flight in 1903, and behind which is the island of Roanoke, where Sir Walter Raleigh made his first experimental settlement in America in the 1580s. I could add "Sacred" and describe Jerusalem, where the Church of the Holy Sepulchre, the Temple, and the Dome of the Rock all sit under the same bloody sun, glinting with passion and all the strife that has passed between them. In the order of descending scale used in this book, "Experiment" would go last, in the part called "Topography." "Sacred" would go after "Utility," in the part called "Chorography." *Geography* is global. *Chorography* is regional. *Topography* is local.

I am glad to be writing at the turn of a century, when change is a feature of everyone's agenda. The strategy of turning the land to profit that has prevailed for so long is being reviewed; this book is my contribution to that review.

———   —

The research for these essays was assisted by a grant from the Graham Foundation for Advanced Studies in the Fine Arts, Chicago, whose director, Richard Solomon, I should like to thank for his help. Thanks also to Roger Conover of the MIT Press for his enthusiasm and support, and thanks to Ann Twiselton of the MIT Press's London office for hers. I am indebted to Manuel De Landa, J. K. Galbraith, Mark Simmonds, Rodney Place, Svetlana Alpers, and Ken Taylor for specific insights. And to everyone who recognizes parts of themselves in the mouthpieces of my dialogues, thanks *and* apologies.

THE CULTIVATED WILDERNESS

La Plaine Morte, Crans-Montana, Switzerland. Photo Darbellay—C. H. Martigny.

1
WILDERNESS

The wilderness is not a landscape you visit; it is all around you, wherever you are. The six short pieces that make up this chapter are separate but related. They are intended as a primer for the descriptions of landscapes that follow, but even more, they stake out the subject matter of this book: the ways in which we humans tussle with the wilderness and change it to suit ourselves.

WILDERNESS

Crammed in, the five of us are, to a wooden bench on the open-air terrace of a restaurant halfway up a snow-covered mountain. The place is as packed as the Airbus 320 we flew in on yesterday. We cruised through the wild stratosphere praying that the software in the flight control computers wasn't stuck in glitch mode. The restaurant terrace is crowded and we are all bulked out by skiwear—two reasons why we feel crammed in—plus this meal we are eating, bread soaked in kirsch and covered in melted cheese, takes a lot of bending to the plate. It is hard to catch the tendrils of Gruyère as they harden in the freezing air. We are on the slopes of Mont Gelé, in the Canton Valais, Switzerland. Laid out before us is the valley of the river Dranse, and the horizon, ten kilometers away, is a three-thousand-meter ridge of limestone crag, a dangerous wilderness of gut-spilling precipices and plummeting falls, all smothered in snowdrifts fathoms deep that have been blown as smooth as skin by the wind. The distance glistens in the sun, and way beyond it the sky is streaked with vapor trails.

The restaurant is called La Marmotte, after an alpine groundhog that hibernates in the winter months, so no one who skis there has ever seen one. I am the only one who cares about this; my friends are engrossed in watching the people crammed into the table next to us. Two tanned, blonde French women are being fed elaborate pickup lines by two tanned and burly South African men. It's like watching animals. The men have no other tongue besides English to use but Afrikaans, which, in Viv's opinion, makes everyone who uses it as attractive as a warthog. She says this in Italian, to keep it secret. It's like the Tower of Babel, this place. All the time more and more skiers are turning up, breathing hard, fresh faced and exhilarated from the downhill swoop, stamping across the terrace in their huge plastic boots like Robocops. Everyone scans everyone else for sexual frisson. The restaurant has a big wooden roof, with expensive-looking copper rainwater pipes, and the Swiss flag flaps cheerfully on a pole on the ridge. Viv explains that it's not there just as decoration. When the blizzard comes down, if you are caught by it and trapped out here, the flag is your signal of refuge. It could save your life.

After lunch we click back into our skis and move off in the direction of the home run, toward the resort town far below. There must be four hundred chalets down there, none of them more than thirty years old. We are in the oldest democracy in the world, but this part is as new as Simi Valley. The best time to see it is at night, on the way to the nightclub, when the neon lights in the shop windows cast a million colors on the snow, and the lights on the ski-lift terminals, high up on the mountain, seem to be bright stars hanging in the sky. It's so black out there in the beyond it makes you shiver. You'd swear you could hear wolves howl.

That's our life in the bourgeois heartland of the ski resort. Shopping, flirting, wrapping our faces in fur, and toasting our downhill runs in *Gluwein*. Further downhill still, one hundred meters below the town and sitting on the springtime snow line, is the old village from which the resort takes its name, although the new village is now many times the size of the original. In the resort, the chalets look like they're made of wood, but in fact they're concrete, overclad in yellow pine six-by-twos. They're apartment blocks, not chalets. Here in the old village are the real Swiss chalets, log cabins as black as smoke, clustered together so close you couldn't get a Porsche between them. The whole place reeks of cows, which live on the ground floors of these buildings all winter, lending their smelly heat to the human occupants upstairs.

I came across one of the village people sawing wood one morning when I was making my way on foot down the mountain to see the valley floor. Downhill work on these forty-five-degree Alpine slopes is breathtaking, and I had stopped to admire the view and to give my heart a chance to slow down. He put down his saw and came over to me, pulling a small bottle out of his pocket. His face was as brown as milk chocolate and covered in creases. He poked the bottle at me in welcome and laughed—and when he laughed all his features compressed in the middle of his face until they looked like crosshairs on a target. *Go on!* his smile seemed to say, *Hit me!* He wanted to sell me something. He peeled back the sleeve of his coat and his lower arm was thick with watches. It looked as though he had a stainless steel gauntlet up to his elbow. I looked more closely and saw the names: Casio, Seiko, Accurist. I remember, in school, learning the secret of Swiss watchmaking. It was that they spend the winter, when the landscape is locked shut by deep snow for months, screwing tiny mechanisms together, with a patience that is exclusive to them. Now here was one of them offering me watches that were made in air-conditioned factories on the Pacific Rim. I wanted to ask him if he knew the English expression "taking coals to Newcastle," but my French wasn't up to it.

I hinted that I would be back later with my friends, and I trudged on down the steep hillside reflecting on that little Swiss theme, the theme of patient settlement in the wilderness, and I realized that even though world trade had washed across the globe and taken Casios to Geneva, things are still as they were and ever will be. Wherever we live, from Jericho to Munich, from Jalalpur to Central Park East, we are nestled in the middle of wilderness. We persuade ourselves that our taming of the world is profound, we lay water mains and sewers and read thousand-year-old books, we drive our autobahns through solid rock, we huddle together in caves lit by the incandescence of television screens. We do everything we can to be safe, and still the planet spins, the winds roar, the great ice caps creak and heave, the continental plates shudder and bring cities crashing to the ground, the viruses infect us and the oceans toy with us, lapping against the edges of our precious land. We are in the midst of wilderness, even curled up with our lovers in bed—and we are not the only living things in this peril.

THE MOST DANGEROUS ANIMAL IN THE WORLD

At the zoo, as a boy, I used to skip from cage to cage marveling at the ferocious smells and the brown stained teeth of all the animals. I thought it wonderful that the big gorilla had been in his little cage since before I was born, and that some of the parrots had been chained to their perches for thirty-five years. I never saw the cruelty. In those days you were still allowed to poke slivers of carrot through the steel nets that enclosed the antelopes and to hurl bread at the bears in their concrete pit. One day I went into the big-cat house with my sister, who had just turned fourteen. As soon as she stepped through the door, one of the tigers sprang up and bounded around his cage trying to get at her. Then he reared up, rampant and magnificent, and roared. She retreated, fast, out of the building, and he calmed down; she came back in and off he went again. There was a bloody raw leg of mutton on the floor of his cage, which he had stopped chewing because he wanted to eat her instead. It was like love at first sight—she was flattered—it was scary. Elsewhere in the zoo, there was a mirror set up with a notice underneath: "You Are Looking at the Most Dangerous Animal in the World!" I was eight. I thought that that tiger was the most dangerous animal in the world. I looked in the mirror at a little boy with clouds of blond curls and cheeks like Cupid. Dangerous animal? It took me a while to figure out what the notice meant.

Years later I heard about a tribe of chimpanzees in which one of the older females had turned serial killer. She pretended to help nurse the babies of the younger females, but in fact she was taking them off to a quiet corner of the woods and bashing them to death. No one among the chimps could figure out what was happening: there are no forensics in chimpanzee life. So humans are not the only ones who kill their own species. There are spiders who eat their mates and king lions who kill the male cubs in their pride to eliminate competition—so what is it that is so dangerous about humans? Is it that they lay waste to ground? The *wilderness* is what was there before the humans came. The *wasteland*—which was once the same thing—is now something else: cultivation gone feral.

The wasteland has become the backdrop for a lot of contemporary imaging: shattered buildings filled with junkies and urban deserts overrun by crime. Why? Is it dismay at the spectacle of liberal democracy falling apart? Is it a fear of the unschooled voices unleashed by that democracy? Or is it merely the version of civilization that requires the least effort?

────────── THE CULTIVATED WILDERNESS ──────────

Back in England, four hundred years old, are the ruins of Kirby Hall. The house was built in a hollow in agrarian Northamptonshire, miles from anywhere. It is one of those exquisite seventeenth-century cultivars that look like ships, cruising out of ancient times and into the modern. A long line of Sir Charles Hattons had it. The first Sir Charles was knighted by Queen Elizabeth for his dancing. They said he had *feet like a golden goat.*

The gardens at Kirby are formal, at their best when full of bees and doves and tulips. At the side of the house, running down toward a little crook, is where the fourth Sir Charles planted what he called his *Wilderness*. It had in it one of every species of English tree—it was a sort of garden poem about England. He called it the Wilderness because it was representative of everything that was outside the garden.

Those Stuart days were full of cultivation. Eighty miles away, in Derbyshire, Hatton's contemporary Cavendish was experimenting with horses, cultivating their nature into the unhorselike movements of the dressage with his eight-foot-long sharp pointed canes. Three thousand miles away, on the edge of the new continent of North America, the first European settlements were budding in a wilderness so full of trees it would have made the fourth Sir Charles faint clean away with envy. Those first settlements in the Virginian wilderness were as perfectly balanced in material as the palaces the settlers left behind them in Europe were balanced in time. The buildings were built out of the trees cut down to make room for them. They were like space stations, tiny glimmers of life support in the huge blacknesss of ancient forest. In Europe, the wilderness was already reduced to enclaves, surrounded by cultivation. Out in Virginia, in 1645, it was still the other way around.

I have an ex-friend who lives in Tucson, Arizona. He calls it *Arid-Zone-a.* I call him an ex-friend because I stayed loyal to his former wife when he split for the United States, but I still miss him. He is *unformal.* Sloppy people, you get lots of. Deliberately unformal people are as rare as people who settle invoices on the due date. He is in love with the gas-station/fast-food/motel/interstate landscapes of the modern Western world. He agrees they are trite—"I'll give you trite," he says—but points out the triteness of other worldwide contemporaneities, like the concrete-block/street-trader/dust-road/Toyota landscapes of the modern African world. Other people might call these landscapes degenerate—call them *wastelands*—but he is so modern, he says that although it is interesting what shape things are, it doesn't matter.

"Beauty is in the eye of the beholden," he says, maintaining that form means nothing to him. He listens to Beethoven symphonies with the CD player switched into shuffle mode. He once showed me a map of Arizona, where it butts up against the Mexican border. The whole landscape between Yuma and

Tucson, an area the size of Vermont, say, or indeed of Switzerland, is divided into four huge land parcels: the Luke Air Force Range, the Cabeza Pieta National Wildlife Refuge, the Organ Pipe Cactus National Monument, and the Papago Indian Reservation. What are these places? Are they preserved wildernesses, segregated from the creeping mold of cultivation? Or is it that the automobile development patterns themselves are a kind of wilderness and the preserved lands are huge gardens, single-use paradises, set down in the wilderness like Eden? On one hand, I say wilderness; on another, I say cultivation. Brought together, palm to palm, they fit each other perfectly. It is hard to see where one starts and the other leaves off—although we must try, or no one will know what to do next.

First of all, I am saying that the wilderness is everywhere. Not just in the oceans, not just in the deserts and the mountain ranges, but everywhere. It trickles down the staircase of the minaret and into the prayor hall of the great mosque at Damascus. It seeps through the filters of the air-cooling plants at Rockefeller Center. But at the same time, I am saying that the whole world now is cultivated and bears the marks of it. High on Everest, Snickers wrappers nestle in the snow. Plastic bottles ride the Gulf Stream. Radio waves, carrying coded messages, cascade across the atmosphere.

Some people say that the old difference between art and nature has been so overwhelmed by the universal cultivation of the global economy that no difference remains. The landscape of the earth is a "single surface," the argument goes, made up of nature and artifice, in indistinguishable convolution. What they're describing is the culmination of the nineteenth-century landscape strategy of industrial exploitation of the earth, which is still the unspoken strategy behind almost all contemporary land development. Other people—academic opponents of the single-surface people—maintain that the previous landscape strategy, the eighteenth-century landscape of the natural picturesque, is a reviewable alternative. They say, "Picturesque? Of course! It is a complete picture of the world." It describes urban forms as well as rural, it has a politics of taxation in it, it has a relation to rational agriculture, and it has a unified source of material, too, in the neoclassical world.

Before there were any humans, the world was in a state of wilderness. Now we have spread out and multiplied; our works have gotten everywhere. A variable ratio of cultivated land to wilderness is present at every spot, with the expanse of the ocean—call that a single surface?—weighting the ratio in favor of wilderness. For the entire twentieth century we have relied on politics to shape the world. We have thought that social planning would make us a new landscape, but we never reckoned on the power of the machines to make landscapes we didn't anticipate. Wham! go the Howitzers. Zoom! go the Jumbo Jets. Click Click! goes the Internet. The point of dwelling on landscape now, at the end of a century when the question asked right at the beginning—*What is appropriate?*—is still unanswered, is to re-perceive the ratio of wilderness to cultivation and research the strategies. There is only one way to do that—it is to go out into the landscape and take a good, long, hard look at it. The point is to replace the guttering candles of the neoclassical world with something less destructive than the furnaces of the nineteenth century.

"And dim the fluorescent tubes of the twentieth?" says my Arizona ex-friend. "Give me a break!"

I once did an experiment to see what happened when I looked long and hard at something obvious in the landscape. I decided to photograph the fourteenth-century cathedral at Ely, in the flatlands of East Anglia, England, from points around a circle centered on the lantern tower. Five concentric circles, in fact, starting with one a mile from the cathedral and finishing with one five miles away.

When the cathedral was first built, it and the little city that clings to it were surrounded by marshland. The Isle of Ely is a greensand hump that stands about fifty feet above the clay of the marsh bed. Fifty feet is not much—five times the height of a basketball net—but because of the flatness of the surrounding land, now drained and called fens and growing onions and radishes by the million, views of the building can be obtained for miles. With a little elevation, such as you get on the dikes of the big ditches that were dug by Dutchmen three centuries ago—that's three centuries after the cathedral was finished—the towers of the building can be just made out, by naked eye, ten miles away.

Ely is an old market city. Eight roads from the surrounding farmland converge on it like spider's legs. The project I was there for consisted of tracing out along one of these roads, taking a photograph centered on the cathedral at every milestone for five miles, then crossing over to the next road and tracking in, again taking a photograph at every mile—and so on, all around the compass. I did it with a friend who is as perceptive of the landscape as Maria Callas was of musical phrase. She says landscape is a series of incidents coming into being, too slowly for us to see, like plants growing. She talks so softly that if you buy an ice cream for her from a roadside van, you can't hear what she wants above the roar of the refrigerator. She sat in the passenger seat of the car whispering her bons mots and hanging onto the grab handle as if she were on a motorbike. We ended up that day with about forty photographs, having covered an area of about eighty square miles.

We talked as we went, driving down the drainage-ditch-lined roads and past the poor little farmhouses, with their woodstained doors and net curtains and rusting machinery in the yards. I tried to explain my idea of thematic landscapes. "We know what theme parks are," I said, "they're full of narratives and thrills—but if we look at the parks instead of the theme, what do we get? Cement grottos, miniature copies of New Orleans, and rapid-river rides. Now think about a park— a landscape—where the theme is not a cute peg to hang a turnstile on, but a feat of perception, a striking of position, that sets up further possibilities of action."

"You've been reading Tao strategy manuals again," she said, catching on immediately. A theme is a position inside a strategy. The industrial exploitation strategy and the antiquarian picturesque strategy are not the only ones, just the most obvious.

My soft-voiced friend, however, was not convinced. When I told her the names of some of my themes—*Unity, Hope, Nation*—she said they sounded like the Nazi Party. When I told her that my idea of wilderness is really landscape without humans, she called me cold-hearted.

"There is no landscape without humans. Never has been. You don't *get* landscape until you get humans," she said. She is steeped in theories of being, and she meant that human relations with the land are centered on simply being in it. I don't agree. I think it's action that matters, which is why I was banging on about strategy. I was of the opinion that if I did roll the car into the ditch—or better still, if I crashed headlong into this articulated agricultural gas-oil tanker hurtling toward us, if I did kill us both and terminate our being—the wilderness would still be there, little changed, cradling our bodies as it does the fallen leaves in November.

"Mind that truck!" she suddenly yelled, with a volume I never knew she had in her. She was sitting up as straight as a hare.

We were coming up to the four-mile circle. The sun was out, the sky was blue, the little clouds enhanced the view, and we edged our way across the fens, stopping every five minutes to clamber out of the car, set up the tripod, focus on the cathedral, snap the shutter, and move on. The activity gradually rescued us from our quarrelsome mood.

We discovered two things out there in the fens. The first is that in the distance, the cathedral spires have a sort of gusty flat presence, like the mirage of greatness. But then, at about one and three-quarter miles out, the cathedral suddenly jumps into full detail and seems instantly to be much bigger—the greatness made real. At that critical distance all the finials and carving and buttressing of Gothic detail suddenly become clear, and mass is swapped for detail. I think that is the distance Gothic buildings are set up for. They are pitched at people walking toward them in the surrounding countryside. There is a pull to it, like wind catching the sails, which puts excitement into the last three thousand yards of the journey.

Just inside this threshold, the new Ely bypass road swings past the city, cutting clean across the old radial roads as it does so. These fast-traffic highways are connected like a huge net across the country and are laid over an older net of smaller detail, which consists of market towns like Ely, with their dependent villages and surrounding farms. I should call the old net a web, because of its time-woven quality. Net? Web? This is not about the bitstream, remember, but human settlement. The new net of fast highways has its own systems, its shopping malls and gas station eateries, its industrial parks and housing estates—you can spend all your time on one circuit and never touch the other. This is the second discovery: what the net and the web have in common is a series of ancient nodes—the old seats of privilege—that have found a new use as recreational centers. These places were built in open country in manorial relation to the web but are now connected by the net into a thing called *heritage*. Their function as connectors between something old and something new is what the heritage fuss is about. It's why the old things have to be restored to an authentic narrative—so they can be made new. *Restoration* is a theme in a strategy, and the strategy is to cling to the past with all the strength that modern methods can muster. *Authenticity* is the science lurking in the nostalgia.

My uncompromising friend calls this strategy despicable. "Treating space like precious metal. Sickening." It is, for her, another example of the *wasteland*. She feels the same about the heritage industry as she does about Whopper burgers. I am more phlegmatic. In the Ely Cathedral lady chapel, the final point of our journey, the recent restoration project involved the installation of new leaded glass. Instead of pictures of Jesus, the glass bears the logos of, among others, the National Westminster Bank and Tesco supermarkets PLC—the sponsors of the restoration.

The exercise at Ely was fruitful, even though the practice of it, the plodding from milestone to milestone around a geometrical grid, was as rudimentary as agriculture. No action, you see—no impulse to greatness—all work. Could we have studied Xanadu by this stick-and-plod method? I ask myself. Or could we have even laid out Jaipur the pink city, the pink *gridded* city, with our eyes so firmly fixed on the ground? I have heard that the bones of the three kings are in a box of everlasting material in the cathedral at Cologne. I have heard of the thousand caves full of silk discovered outside Samarkand, and of the sand turned to glass under the atom bomb testing rigs at White Sands, New Mexico. Bones, stolen silk, sand turned to glass—this is exotica. This is stuff beyond my own nation, but it is all still cultivation. How can I understand it?

J. B. Jackson, the pioneer of landscape studies, proposed that the human history of the land presents us with three distinct landscapes. *Landscape One* was the medieval landscape, where people dwelled in a vibrating, miraculous natural history, held together by tribal affinities and superstition. *Landscape Two* was the neoclassical landscape revivified by the Renaissance and destroyed, after five centuries of fertile inquiry into what the ideal looked like, by—in my opinion—the howitzers of World War I. *Landscape Three* is the loose, inquisitive, and mobile landscape of the modern world, which can be seen, Jackson says, to have similarities to the fragmented and feudal patterns of Landscape One.

I should like to extend this trilogy. Before Landscape One, I want to put a *Landscape Nought,* the time of cave paintings and ice ages, pre–*Homo sapiens,* in which humans are no more equal than the leopards and the chimps. Ahead of us is *Landscape Four,* the fully networked but ethnically fenced-off globe that seems to lie in wait for our grandchildren. Perhaps they will be inspired by their differences and make art as sublime as the paintings of bison in the Lascaux caves.

"Tell me again how everyone used to live in tribes, with chiefs, and used to fight the other tribes to decide where their land ended," says my little friend Alex. "Tell me how they cut off the heads of kings." Alex is six years old, and although his father taught him to ride his bike, I taught him to ride it *fast,* which has bonded him to me. I remember the boy who taught me to run when I was six. He was my best teacher. He took me by the hand and ran so fast I was amazed my legs could keep up—but forever after I knew they could. "Tell me again how they used to fight the other tribes," said Alex. I described for him the slow progress of chiefs into kings, and then kingdoms into nations.

"Tell me again how the trees were planted in the shape of battles." I tried to explain the ideal landscape by describing the park at Blenheim in Oxfordshire.

"Tell me again how the cowboys used to sing to their cows," says Alex. These are the three landscapes, again. The first, in which people lived close to nature; the second, in which they lived in deliberate contradiction to it; the third, in which we live, sustained by our machines, on the surface of it. The cowboy nomads of the high plains were the first inkling of Landscape Three. I told Alex how they crooned to the cattle while the vast herds dozed at night to keep them from panicking and scattering for miles, which they would do at the slightest strange noise—and I reflected how rumor can rush through human society too. A creature going from cultivation into wilderness is called feral. What would you call a creature going the other way, once wild, now tame? The falconers had a name for it. The hawks they had not raised from the egg, but had caught wild and then tamed, were called *haggard*. Feral and haggard: is that what we are? Creatures oscillating between two states? These surroundings of ours, these resultant topographies, these money machines, these forests of advertisement, is this civilization? Or is it something else? Alex considers my questions and draws his eyes down with his hands until he looks like a spaniel. "I don't know," he says, out of his little distorted mouth. "I'm only six."

"One thing's for sure, Alex," I say, hugging his head, "Wilderness is not innocence. It is as wise as the hills."

D O G S

There was a period of a month or two, about a year or two ago, when I studied dogs in my local park, to try and see if what they did about their cultivated state is similar to what humans do. It was about the time that we started seeing news from Bosnia, where it seemed the humans had suddenly turned feral—they had forgotten about the ideas that sustain cultivation and were charging, full tilt, on the road to wasteland. I used to go out in the park every day, dog spotting. My attention first had been drawn by seeing two big poodles, wearing diamanté collars and clipped into topiary shapes, who had knocked over a trash can and were nosing about among the fried chicken leftovers and the soda cans like hyenas—reverting to type. The next day I saw a more complicated scene: two dogs and two men this time. The dogs were both German shepherds. One of the men was a park police officer, with a quilted jacket and a peaked hat and a radio tucked into a holster on his belt. Perfect military creases ran down his trousers, and his hair was cut with a short back and sides. His dog was sleek and well behaved, with a shiny chrome chain around its neck, lying at his feet while he stood and talked to the other man, a creature the opposite of himself: one of the park's tramps, who sat slightly dizzy on a bench, surrounded by plastic bags full of rubbish, with a red face and a gray beard, like Santa Claus fallen on hard times. His dog, the other German shepherd, wasn't sleek and lean like the police dog; it was overweight and out of condition. It was covered in grime and wore a collar made of knotted string. It kept rooting through the plastic bags, while the other dog lay still, patient and good-looking. The two men were laughing and comparing doggy notes.

"Dogs think they're humans," said one of them, "or maybe they think we're dogs—but they don't know what we're up to."

"They don't understand, they just go along with it."

They don't understand why they live in houses and sleep in baskets, or why they get food on plates. They may be happy with the situation, but they don't know why it exists.

It wasn't long before another dog lover arrived to join in. "Talking about dogs!" dog lovers think. "Lovely! Quick! Join in!" She was a woman well into her seventies, with a beautiful head of cream-white hair and a face full of red veins and a huge smile, which flashed out and lit up the scene. Her dog was a great Dane, with a gray hide splashed with maroon blotches. It looked like a Navajo map of the world.

"Dogs may be happy with the situation, but they don't know why it exists," she explained. "They're not *civilized*, they're *domesticated*." I could not help wondering: How many humans are simply domesticated? Living in our civilization—our *cultivation*—without knowing why it exists?

Pond Life

I once took part in a world awareness event, in which a huge tetrahedral map of the world was laid out across the floor of a big hall. They had used aeronavigational maps at a scale of one to a million, so it was maybe 120 feet across. Two hundred ticket holders turned up, and when you went in they reached in a basket and gave you a nationality—I and thirty-three others got China—and told you to take your shoes off and go sit on the map where your country was. We were jammed into China like eels in a bucket. The twenty-six people who represented India were similarly crowded. In fact the whole of Southeast Asia, Middle Africa, and South America were packed like a rush-hour train. The ten people in Europe and the seven in the United States had room to lounge full-length. The Australian was on his own. When they had us all sitting down, the organizers said, "Okay! Now everyone! We're going to distribute the world's resources—and the food is going to be represented by these loaves of sliced bread. Share it out!" We Chinese got our loaf and we opened it up and shared it out, one slice each. In Africa they got half a loaf and had to divide their slices into pieces. Then all we crowded nations looked up and saw the people in the United States, lounging on the floor. They had been given one whole loaf of bread each! We hated them!

"Okay, now everyone!" said the organizers. "We're going to play a game called world revolution."

Afterward, I walked back home with two of my fellow Chinese, Jack and Jim, across the Heath, which is a nine-hundred-acre park in North London. It's called the Heath because it's a wild park—land that was not built on during the London buiding boom of the 1860s because of a technical obstruction in the will that passed possession of it down the generations. The nineteenth-century suburbs stop abruptly at the edge, as deck chairs on a crowded beach stop at the sea.

"There's a place in Bombay that is a wilderness in the city," said Jim. "A patch of jungle on a hill, where tigers roam and vultures circle overhead—a secret place, a forbidden garden, a burial ground, with a huge unclimbable wall all around. The people leave dead bodies at the gate, and priests creep out at night to take them in and lay them out on stone slabs under the sky for the vultures to strip to the bone."

"Which came first," asked Jack, "the city or the park? The wilderness or the garden?"

The Heath rises gently from all sides to peak at a hill in its center, from which the whole city can be seen, spread out like a pat of cultivation across the old floodplain of the river. We walked on up there and saw the dust of demolition sites rising like mist against the horizon. More clouds, more sky, a whole hemisphere full. The evening springtime sun lit everything like a stage set. The last big passenger plane of the day hove into view, like a beast with its nostrils flaring, and its wings as stiff as a butterfly pinned to a board. It laid the whine of its racing compressors like a wave before it, as though it was surfing on its own din, the engine fan tips spinning faster than the speed of sound and adding thousands of little sonic booms to the roar of the jet efflux. It was beautiful. It banked across the clouds, gray and glinting and solid, and cruised off into the distance, carrying its fragile cargo toward a strip of concrete thirty miles away.

A solitary crow took to its wings and flapped off into a tree. It was gripping some cheap confection in its beak, some raspberry bonbon. It was cawing with pleasure, as though it had found the ultimate berry. Two American spaniels stood up there on the hill nose to nose, with their glamorous tan curls backlit by the sun, looking like miniature buffalo. There was a woman in a sleeping bag, too, right out in the open, slumbering on the grass with her belongings beside her in a supermarket bag. Her red hair glistened with the evening damp. When we passed, she opened one eye and winked at us, like a crocodile. It is beautiful, the park: full of strange lives—equal to Luxor, and to the whole Nile Valley from Alexandra to the cataracts, even though everything is commonplace and not filled with the clash of the swords of kings.

We turned onto the path that runs alongside the six large ponds that drain the hill. They are laid out one after the other, each one spilling into the next through an underground culvert, the last of which discharges into the sewers of the city. Each pond is big enough to land a gaggle of geese on, or indeed to drown a company of fully armed soldiers: the ponds are almost lakes. At the top of the path the first pond takes water from the spring streams and gathers it behind a dam, which is fenced stoutly to keep the anglers away from the fish and the dogs away from the toads. From there, the other five ponds descend the slow slope for about a mile, through woods, past playing fields and vistas, each one fed from the one before and feeding the one below.

Next below the fish pond is a bathing pond, for women bathers only, hedged with hazel thickets to keep out leering males. Below the women's pond is a bird sanctuary, pond number three, full of ducks and geese. This one has an iron railing and is set aside for nesting. It has marshy reeded banks and old tree stumps standing in the water. The Canada geese who live there are big birds with black heads and white chin straps. They have given up migrating in favor of the easy pickings they get in the park: they have joined the human race. In a couple of months their little goslings will be begging for food, too, flapping their infant wings like thumbnails covered with silver fur.

The fourth pond is where model boats are sailed on weekends. Not sailed, in fact, but driven hard, *full throttle,* and people gather to giggle at the boyish stubbornness of the boaters. The fierce little boats scream around the pond, just skimming the surface, with a smell of burned cabbage from the vegetable oil in their engines hanging in the air, until, with a sudden influx of spray in the fuel line, they stop and wallow, silent, like sulking teenagers; and the boaters pull on long boots and wade out to get them back. Pond five is the men's bathing pond, surrounded by hawthorn blossom and weeping willows, and last of all is the low pond, the muddy one, which has a sort of beach made of mud, from which dogs swim out after sticks their owners hurl for them.

Dogs, men, boats, ducks, women, fish, I said to myself. It was a sort of incantation to say in time to my stride as we passed the six ponds. "Dogs, Men, Boats, Ducks, Women, Fish," I said aloud. It's a simple list, but it could cover everything. It could cover all that our landscapes are made of: civilization, humanity, *nature*. We walked up from the bottom pond to the top, and when we reached the fish pond the wind had dropped and I undid my coat and pushed the collar away from my cheeks. The surface of the pond was flat and smooth, and impenetrably green. Every so often it was broken by the pinging ripple of a fish nabbing a surface-walking fly. The water showed dark green in the shadows and light green under the sky, but it was all green. The low evening sunlight picked up a world of detritus lying on the surface: motes of dust, a few leaves already turned yellow and fallen before the year had really begun, a chocolate bar wrapper drifting in the breeze, all red and gold and white like the sails of the *Santa Maria*. Underneath this still, calm surface, there was a wilderness, a world unvisited by human beings, where everything went on as it always had, the species of pond life wrapped in their battles for survival, held in balance by the ferocity of the struggle. The real evolutionary battle, right there, in the park in the middle of the city.

I
GEOGRAPHY

Planet earth from Apollo 17, December 1972. Courtesy National Aeronautics and Space Administration.

2

UNITY

The Seven Wonders of the World

A line can be drawn around a piece of territory, and all the things inside the line described and remembered. What happens when the territory is so big it covers the world?

UNITY

The Seven Wonders of the World

———————— Archeology ————————

The ground is yellow, the sky is blue. If you were an oil painter, you would mix plenty of viridian with the cobalt to match the shock of the turquoise on the horizon. You'd start with raw amber to catch the antelope-hide color of the grass, although the intensity of light in the Gulf might defeat you: there's so much gray in it. We are in Iraq. The river Euphrates creeps past in the background, seeping through the reeds, and will maintain this biblical pace for another three hundred miles, until it reaches Basrah and the sea. The flood plain of the Euphrates is one of the first places in the world to be cultivated. It makes *Old Man River* Mississippi look like a little kid.

The big square pool of water in the center of the site is black and brackish, fringed with reeds and decorated with a constellation of white egrets. On three sides of the square a hump of baked-clay bricks, smoothed out by centuries of erosion, frames the pool into an amphitheater. It is the site of ancient Babylon. The derelict remnant before us might be three times as old as Methuselah. It might have been built twenty-seven hundred years ago—it might be the remains of the Hanging Gardens of Babylon, one of the Seven Wonders of the World.

The Egyptian Hall, the British Museum, London. Photograph by the author.

Off to the south, still in Iraq, stands the great ziggurat of the Sumerian city of Ur. It is even older than Babylon: four thousand years old. The British archeologist Leonard Woolley, who went there in the 1920s, called it the Mound of Pitch, because its bricks are stuck together not with mortar but with pitch—a material that, even when as ancient as this, glints freshly black and blue when you crack it open. Woolley went to Ur with an Oxford University expedition, dressed in tweeds and safari shorts and half-skin brogue shoes. He dug down into the clay of the floodplain looking for evidence of the Old Testament and found the brick remains of the ancient city of Ur and exposed them to the light and dusted them down and mapped the streets using names from Oxford—Carfax and Church Lane, Gay Street and Straight Street—and he and his companions wound sheets around themselves and posed for photographs, pretending to shop and cook and gossip in the streets just as they would have done in Ur all those thousands of years ago. But the mound of pitch is *not* one of the Seven Wonders of the World.

You can do archeology at almost any spot on earth. You can dig down and find the accoutrements of old lives buried in the dirt along with the worms and the centipedes. Try it in your own backyard: peg out the ground and dig down systematically, carefully recording the details of everything you find.

"Hey look! A Tonka Truck! In far from perfect condition!" It is nothing less than the proof of past lives. But looking into the past is a tricky thing. As you retreat in time, the evidence becomes so scanty and so contaminated by the process of being passed down the generations that you can be sure about nothing. Archeologists, like historians, have become exquisitely conscious of the distortions they deal with. They will not admit to conclusion, being aware of their human tendency to shape the evidence to fit their own preconception. Archeologists now are not like Leonard Woolley. They refuse to separate subject and object even when they are dealing with lumps of stone, even though they would bruise them-selves if they dropped one of these lumps on their toes.

"That shows how much you know," said the archeologist. "We don't dig anymore. With the survey equipment we have today, we can investigate the site without even breaking the ground." When I met her she was measuring statues in the British Museum and logging the coordinates into her laptop. She calls herself a *virtual archeologist.* "In any case," she went on, "what we are looking for now is evidence of life-style, not monuments"—in other words, the people, not the kings—"we are more interested in examining the contents of the turds in the midden than in finding the keystones of the palace."

I had gone to the British Museum with my friend Sally. We had walked through halls filled with the bulging biceps and the gorgeous nostrils of giants carved by Egyptians from Nile Valley granites. The apocalypse-sized torsos aroused my pre-occupation with the way time is locked into the land, as in the expression "as old as the hills." I voiced my prejudice—that archeology is a process of digging down to expose the past in the present, to make a subterranean honeycomb of past efforts for us to wander in, amazed, like tourists in a time machine.

"There is no past and no future," I said, "only the present. All this stuff, all this evidence of past action, these carved stones, that's in the present, too. It all exists with us, in the present, now."

Sally protested: she said that it sounded too much like me-dieval tapestry. She said that it is living that mitigates time-lessness—and that it's memory that explains it. "It's the way human lives overlap that produces history," she said. "The way that memories are passed on from old ones to young ones."

Each generation sees the same world but sees it with different eyes. It is easy to sympathize with the aboriginal inhabitants of the Mississippi-Ohio confluence when they protest at the plunder of their ancestral burial grounds and at the bones' being sold to tourists. It is easy to understand the desire of the people of Athens to retrieve the Elgin Marbles from the British Museum, London, and fix them back up on the frieze of the Parthenon, Athens.

"It's a hole torn in their history, to have them here and not there," Sally said. But the British Museum is full of stuff like that. Old-fashioned, objective archeology. The British empire lasted five generations, from Clive to Kitchener, in which the British invented a unity called *we-own-the-world.* "The sun never sets on the empire," they said, meaning not that it would last forever but that it spanned the globe. The British Museum is their collection cabinet—what is in the museum is the swag of the British empire's archeologists. Big precious stones hauled out of holes in the ground. Egyptian heads with lips as big as billboards and fists like battering rams. Assyrian stone lions covered with cuneiform letters as thick as fur. What should we do? Take it all back where it came from and insert it carefully back into the ground?

"Sure, why not?" said the virtual archeologist. "Just make sure you get it all on disk before you disperse it."

It turned out that *no past, no future* is what she thought, too. She had a sort of hard-disk analogy for memory in which bodies of evidence can be flung like frisbees from one corner of the world to another. There is no whispering in the ears of little children—it is all protocol.

"Everything online means no place and no time," she said. Sally looked so pissed off. "Everything online means no place and no time," she echoed disgustedly. "But what else is archeology if not place and time?" she asked, her face busted with disbelief.

The archeologist gazed back with a glittering blue stare. Her eyes looked like Delftware. Her face was as flawless as one of the statues on the frieze behind her. Her hair was ice-blonde. We were talking to her in the shadow of a big lime-stone statue of a horse, twice life-size, whose hindquarters had been lost, as if shot away by a cannon. Its bit and harness were modeled in bronze, gently staining its chin green with leeched-out copper. The statue came from the top of the Mausoleum of Halicarnassus—which was one of the Seven Wonders of the World.

Halicarnassus was a city that's now called Bodrum, in Turkey, where the Knights of St. John built their castle in the fifteenth century. The Mausoleum was a tomb, and its name—the generic for all big, showy tombs—comes from the name of the man whose body was interred there, King Mausolos. The Mausoleum was a white marble pyramid, encrusted with statues and regimented with columns. It stood on the hill overlooking Halicarnassus, its immaculate detail as sharp as a cutter against the jumble of mud houses the city was made of. My guess is that it had the same sort of presence as the Taj Mahal—white marble, decorated all over, roughly the same bulk, too, and built for love, like the Taj, by a spouse who died before it was finished. How unfortunate it is that these great things, these Wonders of the World, were built in earthquake country! The Mausoleum stood for fifteen hundred years, but by the time the Knights of St. John built their castle across the harbor, the place was a ruin. The knights needed a supply of finished blocks of stone—and there it was. The more they dug down into it, the more there was. Great blocks of green pumice from the core of the tomb for the walls, and masses of limestone statues that could be first admired for their exacting qualities and then broken up and ground down to make mortar. Eventually, excitedly, they came across the jewel-charged burial vault of Mausolos himself, right down at the bottom of the building, and they exposed it to daylight—and to the plunder of thieves.

The few statues that survived are now in the British Museum, and it is these that the virtual archeologist was logging onto disk. She told us that the sculptors who made the statues, 350 years before Christ, had one priority: accuracy. The painters of the time had it, too. It was like voodoo to them. She told us about the painter Appelles, who could paint grapes so real that birds would try to eat them.

"The statues at Halicarnassus were so accurate, we can measure the stone flesh and reconstruct the skull profiles," she said. "Like those reconstructions of murdered people, you know the ones? Built up in clay on exhumed skulls? Well, like those, in reverse."

I tried to imagine her own perfect flesh being peeled off her skull.

"But what are you doing it *for*?" said Sally. "What's the point?"

"It's the archeology of human form," she said, "and who needs museums? It's all in here." She held up a little blue plastic floppy.

"Come on, Sally," I said. "Say yes to the world! It's a good idea!"

I wanted to stay and learn more about the Seven Wonders of the World. *Why seven?* I wanted to know. *Why there and then?* And, because there is past and no future, *Why now?*

"Have you heard of Michael Psellus?" the archeologist asked me, tunneling into me with those truthful eyes. "He was the chronicler of Byzantium, a thousand years ago, same time as William the Conqueror. He had a little concrete block, made of pieces from each of the Seven Wonders of the World ground down to dust and mixed with cement," she said. "He used it as a paperweight."

"Where is it now?" I asked her. I really wanted to see it. "Is it here in the museum?"

The Seven Wonders of the World are a symbol of unity. The world they were the wonders of is the empire of Alexander the Great—who, by force of charisma, amalgamated all the ancient civilizations of the world into one thing: the first landscape unity. He married the energy and intelligence of Greece with the luxury and power of the Orient. And now here is this little block of cement, the keep-it-in-your-pocket version of Alexander's empire.

"Where is it now?" I repeated, and she laughed. "It's so easy!" she exclaimed. "Perhaps he dropped it and it smashed to pieces. Perhaps I made it up."

"You can fool all of the people some of the time," said Sally, her face a picture of storms. "And you can fool some of the people all of the time." She was striding through the galleries toward the exit so fast that schoolchildren scattered before her like sparrows. "But," she went on, apparently assuming that I did not know the punch line, "you can't fool all the people all of the time."

"Naive! Sally! Those you can't fool, you kill!" I was hoping to bounce her out of her rage by saying something daft. She stopped and whirled around so fast I crashed into her. "The trouble is," I pressed on, "when you start killing them, they change their minds and say they believe you after all."

She looked at me long and hard, breathing like a bull. "Forget it," she said. *Authenticity* is a difficult word to say when you're angry, but she said it anyway, stretching the last three syllables into one hissing spit: "Authenticity is as vital to archeology as the time of death is to the homicide squad. And there's that idiot fucking about with it. Press one button and the truth evaporates. Press another and it comes back in a different form."

I have since embarked on a little cement block called *The Cathedrals of England.* I go about scraping stone dust from their crumbling fabrics, and I have my bag of cement ready. Just then, though, I wanted to hear more about Alexander and the Seven Wonders of the World. I watched Sally disappear around the corner, and then I went back to the blue-eyed archeologist and the tomb statues from Halicarnassus.

ALEXANDER

If ever I write a love story, I want the hero to be like Alexander the Great. But no one could be *like* Alexander. My hero will have to *be* Alexander. He will have succulent lips and bronze-

Wrestlers of the Korongo Nuba tribe of Kordofan, Sudan, 1949. Photograph by George Rodger/Magnum Photos.

colored curls and indigo eyes. He'll have a strong neck and legs like springs and a body designed by Zeus—and I'll never sell the film rights because there'll never be an actor born of woman who could play the part.

Alexander was the most charismatic human before Christ. He had a manner that attracted people like fire on a cold night. He had a dangerous temper, but they forgave him because it was *Great Man's Temper,* which is a fury with lesser beings for not attempting to transcend their bodies of clay. When he became king of Macedonia, Alexander, twenty-two years old, picked up his father's ambition to destroy Persia and ran with it so fast that he was over the horizon by the time his own people realized what had happened—that they had conquered the whole wide world.

He was revered for his confidence and his strength and his courage, but it was his optimism that drove him. Before he set out to conquer the kings of the East, he divided his Greek dominions among his friends, and when one of them said, "Why, boy, what will you have left for yourself?" he simply said, "I shall have hope."

Alexander set out on his campaign into Asia in 334 B.C. This was two thousand years after the building of the Great Pyramid at El Gîza, and nearly three hundred after Nebuchadnezzar built the Hanging Gardens of Babylon. It was nearly one hundred years after the statue of Zeus at Olympia had been erected for the eighty-sixth Olympic games, about twenty years after the rebuilding of the Temple of Artemis at Ephesus, and only sixteen after the completion of the Mausoleum at Halicarnassus. Those are five of the Seven Wonders of the World. The other two, the Colossus of Rhodes and the Pharos Lighthouse, had not yet been constructed.

It took ten years for Alexander to conquer Persia and three of the four ancient centers of civilization: the Nile, the Euphrates, and the Indus. The fourth, on the Yellow River in China, another two thousand miles east and fractured by war, could have fallen, had he continued. In the West the infant Roman Empire was slogging it out inch by inch for possession of the peninsula, growing like coral, one bud at a time. Could that have fallen, too? China and Rome were not in Alexander's empire, and neither were the forests of Gaul and the North African fringe of Carthage, but all the rest of the world was. All the ancient territory of the Akkadians and the Sumerians, the Elamites, the Persians, the Medeans, the Bactrians, the Archaemenids, the Amorites, the Hittites, the Phrygians and Lydians, the Parthians and Sasanians, the Athenians, the Thebans, the Spartans and the Corinthians, the Myceneans, the Minoans, the Hyksos, the Egyptians, the Nubians, the Assyrians—all of this ancient land and everything in it, *the Garden of Eden, the Temple of Solomon, the remains of the Ark:* all of it had fallen to Alexander. It was vast, this new world. It took six months to make the round trip from Eschate, in the east, to Sicily, in the west. A trip around the world now, around the whole globe that we know, could be made in two days by jumbo jet. Even if we disqualify the aeroplane and do the journey by boat—the *USS Carl Vinson* perhaps, nuclear powered and cruising at twenty-four knots—it would still take only a month and a half. So it could be said that Alexander's world was four times as big as ours. That's a planet the size of Neptune.

The beautiful Alexander died in Babylon, the year after the end of his campaign. Just like the British, his empire stayed together for five or six generations before losing its coherence and fragmenting, and in that two hundred years there was a cascade of technical discovery. It was the time of the Venus de Milo and the Laocoön. It was when Euclid did mathematics, and Archimedes did mechanics, and Eratosthenes measured the diameter of the earth. What subject should have been more obvious to these occupants of Alexander's world than the physical world itself? Their time has come to be known as *Hellenistic,* but the important thing, the thing on which the idea of the Seven Wonders was founded, is that it was *one world.*

Before he died, Alexander had ordered the building of the Pharos Lighthouse on an island connected to the city of Alexandria by a causeway. It was a beacon in a tower shining out over the Mediterranean: it was the beacon at the center of the Alexandrine world. Four days' sailing north of the city was the Colossus of Rhodes, the biggest statue in a world full of statues. The Colossus was finished in 282 B.C. and the Pharos Lighthouse twelve years later. From that time, all Seven Wonders existed together in the world for just forty years, until the Colossus was bought down by an earthquake. The generation that lived in this forty years was the beneficiary of all the potential in Alexander's new world, and intent on mapping its quality. So what was in it? They looked around them and saw that it was occidental and oriental: it was ancient as well as new. They saw that it stretched back as far as humans went and forward as far as imagination could go. So they asked, *What is in it?* And they saw the Seven Wonders of the World.

The Pyramid of Khufu at Gîza is the only one still standing. There is a piece of its outer casing in the British Museum. There are pieces of the Temple of Artemis, and the broken statues from the Mausoleum. That's three. There are blue-glazed bricks, possibly from the walls of the Hanging Gardens of Babylon, that's four. The Olympian Zeus has been lost completely. It was taken to Constantinople by the Romans and destroyed in a fire, and nothing of it has been found, except for the poignant little terra-cotta molds for its gold dressings, which are in the museum at Olympia. That's five. The bronze Colossus lay broken on the ground for nearly a thousand years after the earthquake brought it down because the Rhodians had been forbidden by the oracle to move it. It was finally sawed up and carted away by Arab traders in 654, and somewhere in the Levant, there may still be things in use—gates, other statues—made from that bronze. That's six wonders: the last is the Pharos Lighthouse, another victim of earthquake, which was finally demolished in the fourteenth century, and its stones used to fortify the Ottoman garrison at Alexandria.

A few days after our meeting in the museum I visited the virtual archeologist in her cellar beneath the shadow of Tyburn. The room was dark, but three big-screen Macs whirred and glowed in the darkness. The screen saver was a fox-hunting scene, where a pack of followers the size of an army jumped a fence over and over. The pixels on the screen cracked with red coats and green grass and the wild yellow eyes of the horses.

Welcome to the house of mirrors! I thought. *What is virtual reality if not a hall of mirrors—witchcraft?*

"What happens if one of them breaks?" I said. "Seven years' bad luck?"

"Oh, they're obsolete long before they break down," she said. "Like people." Her ice-blonde hair was gone and had been replaced by a mat of red curls.

"I like your wig," I said. "Is that virtual?"

"A wig is camouflage, not virtual. There's a difference. There's no narrative in camouflage. And it's the blonde that's a wig. Want to see the program?"

"Sure," I said.

The program was an animated simulation of the Seven Wonders of the World. Like everyone who tries, she had discovered that the description of one damn wonder after another leads to stupefaction. It's the narrow assumptions of the ancient world that do it—assumptions that wear you down with their profundity. Take the Temple of Artemis. The first statue of the goddess was a meteorite, a lump of extraterrestrial stone that was the brother of the *Omphalos* in the Temple of Delphi. The Artemis cult was a long-lived thing that went on for centuries. Later statues of her showed her head emerging from a rough boulder of stone, and still later statues have her as a sort of ornate column with a human head and shoulders and arms and with eighteen breasts hanging from her chest, pendulous, comprehensive, the fountain of all nourishment. They are sensual, gaudy images, with gilded lips and painted faces. Her ceremonies were loud and vivid. The temple building itself was the wonder—but its special character was that it was so animated by the presence of the goddess that it was thought to be alive, actually a living building. Because Artemis was stone herself, she imbued the stones of the building with her own deep quality. So much so, that when the temple was destroyed by the vandals, fragments of stone were taken and worshiped in their own right, like pieces of the flesh of the goddess.

Now, which is more wonderful? The ancient theory that meteorites are gods, or the modern one that they have hurtled through space locked in the ice tails of comets, the remnants of some distant cataclysm, and have survived their journey to earth through the smelting friction of the atmosphere?

"The thing is, to try and compress it all into three minutes." She was serious. "They get it wrong when they say that the three-minute attention span is a function of modern idiocy. Three minutes is the time it takes to perceive something new, which is what modern people are having to do all the time." Her face was glowing in the light of her machinery, and it felt as though we were in the control room of some unofficial weapons system. "Can you imagine it? Centuries of staring at the same thing, then Alexander comes roaring through and changes everything." She shook her head as if it surprised her. "No wonder he went so far. They had lost the power to detect movement, with all that stone staring." She smiled at me and pushed me into a chair. "Nowadays," she said, "new things come up all the time, in one three-minute snatch after another, and the forms of the world appear like mirages—" she paused and waved her hand across her platoon of glowing screens—"in chimeras."

So virtual reality is literature, not physical space. It is the illusion of form and not form itself. What painting used to be, I guess—that's something we can agree on. People who construct virtual landscapes are doing what landscape painters have always done.

The weapons system is switched to action station, the disks are booted up, and we watch the three-minute Seven Wonders of the World.

The Pyramids are not lumps of masonry. They are tiny gilded chambers surrounded by walls so thick they defy comprehension. Tunnels just big enough for a cat to crawl through connect the chambers to the star-filled universe through the mass of the stone walls. Everything explodes: stones fly everywhere like the Big Bang and re-form on a reeded marsh, all slapping together with a billion bricks into layers of hot black tar, where they shimmer blue in a heat haze. Schoenberg's creepy "Song of the Queen's Slave," opus fifteen, fills the air. She came from Iran, land of mountains, like her mistress, and they both pined for home so hard in the flat nothing of the marshes that Nebuchadnezzar built an artificial mountain for them, which was called the Hanging Gardens. The turquoise and umber colors of the desert get more and more intense as dusk falls, and then the sky lights up with a meteor shower, and one of them hits the ground with a blinding impact and throws up stones around it in the shape of a temple. The glowing meteorite transmutes toward the feminine and appears at a window, high up in the gable—the epiphany of Artemis. We are in the temple precinct, slitting open the bellies of black bulls, gutting steaming pink offal into piles and heaving their bodies onto a fire, for the temple is changing into the Temple of Zeus at Olympia. A swarm of athletic black statues sprouts from the ground and chatters for attention like locusts, while the pyramid of bull's ash grows higher and higher and twelve hundred years passes in seconds, three hundred Olympiads of ancient time: through the smoke of the fire the gigantic chryselephantine—*chrysos,* gold: *elephantine,* ivory—statue of Zeus stands up and crashes through the temple roof and strides off across the sea followed by the black-fly swarm of statues.

"You're going to have to change that bit," I say. "Zeus looks like a kid's cartoon. Like Godzilla."

"Wait, watch this," she says.

The swarm of statues crosses the sea and settles like storks around the marble tomb of Mausolos, bright and white as a sail, while the Zeus crashes on across a foaming sea, the spray igniting into molten metal and coating him in bronze as he goes, changing into the bronze Colossus to stand beside the harbor at Rhodes. A brilliant sun grows on the screen, and the statue flashes heliographic signals from his headdress south to the Pharos Lighthouse at Alexandria, its own polished bronze mirror in the roof glinting in the distance like a diamond. To be visible at thirty miles, as Josephus says it was, it must have been five hundred feet high—only half the height of the Eiffel Tower, and indeed only a quarter of the height of the highest thing in the world today, the KTHI TV mast in North Dakota—or is it the Plock TV mast in Poland?—but still, higher than the Great Pyramid, and the highest thing in the world back then.

The screen goes blank, and the roar of jet noise that accompanies the last part stops abruptly.

"What about that?" she says.

"Just one thing," I said, "at the end. Why not go back to the Pharos and visit the deep insides of it? You might find the body of Alexander." When he died, his corpse was snatched from Babylon and taken by Ptolemy to Alexandria, to confirm that place as the center of the Alexandrine world. It was laid to rest in a mausoleum that has never been found. If I were looking for it, I would say, What better place than the base of the lighthouse?

"At the end you could swoop out of the top of the light-house as the beam swings around and illuminates the top of the Great Pyramid, way off in Cairo."

"Yes!" she says, with her cheekbones glinting in the dim light. "The Pyramids all covered in purple smog, with jet trails in the sky above, and everything loops back to the beginning."

PERCEPTION

A month later I am with my friends Sally and Shahriar sitting on the grass in an eighteenth-century English parkland, surveying the little temples and grottoes with which the Palladians attempted to evoke the wonderful ancient world. I have been canvassing people for alternative lists of the Seven Wonders, because of all the original wonders only the Pyramid remains. It is *the* wonder of the ancient world.

"Stonehenge?" says the mystical fogey in his smelly tweeds. "That's as old as the Pyramids."

"The Wisconsin effigy mounds, which look from the air like a zoo full of dinosaurs? Or the great serpent mound of Ohio?" says Brave-as-a-bear, from behind the wheel of his taxicab.

"The Dome of the Rock at Jerusalem?" This one is from Shahriar, who is a Muslim and a Persian—and who never misses an opportunity to remind me that the history of Iran extends further back than the history of England, or that Iranian poetry on an off day is finer than Chaucer and Shakespeare and Coleridge and Auden rolled together.

"And what about Ayers Rock, and the Grand Canyon, and the Ross Ice Shelf in Antarctica? It's *nature* that's wonderful," says Sally.

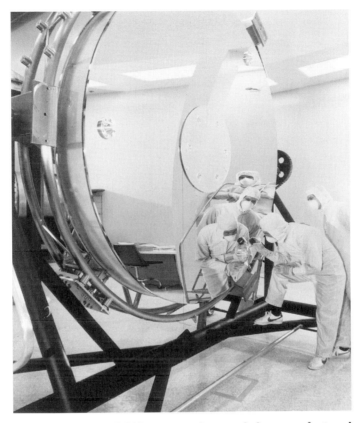

The mirror of the Hubble space telescope being manufactured at Perkin-Elmer, Wilton, CT, January 1984. Courtesy National Aeronautics and Space Administration.

It's like trying to read the Sunday papers. Too much opinion. I insist that the *Seven Wonders of the World* is a figure of landscape unity. All these wonderful things they suggest are outside the territory, or outside the time, or foul of the politics of the Alexandrine world. Sally insists, "It's nature that's wonderful." She thinks she has only to pick the nearest flower and point out its intimate perfection—to put her hand across my mouth and make me listen to the gust of a passing swan's wingbeat—to throw her arms out like a Christian and embrace the vast and colorful sky—to show me herself, even.

"The point is, Sally, the wonders have to be human made. Unity is not the whole world, it's a perception of human civilization. Not the whole world, but one world."

She beckons to Shahriar, who is busy looking at himself in a mirror set into the wall of one of the temples. "For Alexander," she says, "the world stretched to the edges of the empire, from Sicily to the Indus plain. To us, the world is as big as the whole planet earth to the edges of its atmosphere."

Shahriar strikes a pose, and his dark Persian eyes glitter in their purple beds. "Our human representatives on the moon have seen it rising in the black sky over the dust gray horizon, and watched it glowing blue, and felt the finite complexity of it, with every other human being in the universe contained inside, like a nest full of bees. That is our one world."

"Is that what you call Iranian poetry?" I say.

"Exactly," says Sally. "Isn't it beautiful?"

Sally and Shahriar have stuck a crowbar into my definition of unity and levered it open. The unity of the modern world is far greater than Alexander's and far more complex. It's too late to snuff it out, no matter what the fundamentalists do—if knowledge won't hold us together, money will. We are chained together by money like slaves on a slave ship. The future is unknown, possibly terrible, it may all lead to a great war for freedom two generations from now—but it is one world. What are the seven wonders in it? My two friends are magnanimous in victory. They agree there will be nothing on the list that is not human made, and that everything in it will exist in the world in the present moment. They strut around, flirting like pigeons and shouting suggestions.

"The Great Wall of China?"

"Venice?"

"Reims Cathedral?"

"Or the Eiffel Tower?" says Sally, "Or the Statue of Liberty?" She claps her hands and jumps up and down. "Disneyworld!"

There are so many candidates for the seven wonders of the modern world. How can we choose? How is unity perceived? I remember the virtual archeologist and her three minutes. I remember that on the edge of the precipice above Cuzco, at Saqsaywaman, there is an ancient wall made of stones too big for a hundred men to lift, which zigzags across the summit like jagged lightning. Does it, in fact, spell out the name of the god of thunder? That's what perception tells me. My companions are falling over with laughter, saying that *Saqsaywaman* is a song by Roy Orbison, but what about this business of the lightning? Is it just another creative fiction? Is it real or virtual?

If it's hard to perceive the ancient, simple landscapes, it's harder still to see the ground beneath the clutter of the modern world. Not impossible, just difficult. It must be simpler to concentrate on ancient questions such as "What will the sun do next?" or "How many times will I see the moon before I die?" It must be simpler not to have to accommodate Alexander and the Crucifixion and Disneyland and the Vietnam War and Landsat satellites and weigh them all into the equation of perception, but it can be done. *Perception* is an active thing. You need to strike a position, to take a stand on what the conclusion might be before you have it, and therein lies the difficulty. You could be making it all up: it could be *virtual*—it could be literature.

———————

First, a wonder of the world must be human made. Second, it must exist now. Third, it must be tangible, too, and have form of its own. These are the phase-three rules.

Sally's contribution is the Hubble telescope.

"It's as delicate as a daisy and as big as a Mack truck," she says. "It's all precision and control. You know, the primary mirror, eight feet around, is so flat that if it were the size of Australia an ant could step over the highest mountain?"

"How can a concave reflector be flat?" I ask.

"You know what I mean," she says, "flat means level. And, since you bring it up, in orbit the mirror's curve changes because there's no gravity. So they have little servo pistons all around the edge to bend it and focus it again."

The cameras in the Hubble are trained on their objectives for the long exposures needed—hours and hours—by a computer map that locks onto adjacent stars and tracks their slow movement. The telescope is held steady by spinning gyroscopes—its setup is so delicate that it could be thrown out by a tape motor switching on and off in the data recorders, let alone retro rockets. This sensitivity means that it can photograph stellar events at a distance of fourteen billion light years, twenty-four thousand times further than the naked eyes of us on earth.

"And that means seeing things that happened fourteen billion years ago, right out on the edge of the universe!" she says.

"Christ, Sally. It means we can see the origins of the universe, here with us now, in the present!" She looks at me dumbstruck at this awesome proof of the theory of *no past no future*—at which point Shahriar chips in.

"You people with your Coca Cola and your machinery make me laugh," he says. "They are not wonders. A wonder must be permanent. That is why the Pyramids are one of the wonders of the modern world: they alone are still with us."

"Give us the benefit of your wisdom, O great one," says Sally. She puts her arms around his neck, in spite of the sarcasm. She looks as though she's about to kiss him.

"The Ka'aba is of no architectural merit, say the textbooks, and they decline to illustrate it," says Shahriar. He talks as though he is the king of Persia explaining the world to his children. I can see what Sally sees in him. His hair is black as a crow, and his left temple is striped with what looks like a dueling scar. He is charismatic. "The Ka'aba is a ton-meter windowless cube, a shrine, which is covered by a black velvet cloak trimmed with gold. It incorporates in its northeastern corner the black stone, seven inches long, *meteoritic,*" he says with emphasis, "which fell from paradise with Adam: for this is the spot where Adam first worshiped after his expulsion from paradise. The stone was white when it was first given to Abraham, the builder of the shrine, by the archangel Gabriel. It has become black through receiving the kisses of so many sinful men. The wonder of it is not this story, however. It is that the building is a focus for a thousand million people. Every Muslim, wherever he is on the planet, is facing toward this place when he prays."

There it is, the modern world. I might think it is all money and machinery, but it has these two shifts in it: one, the open inquiry of science summed up in the Hubble; the other, the enduring absolutism of holy shrines. Each has a way of saying it can contain the other; by the time we find out which prevails, the world may no longer be modern. Shahriar and Sally are melting into each other.

"I think sex is the wonder of the world," says Sally, and she is not the first to say that.

They leave before I can tell them my wonder. It is a well-rehearsed favorite. The Pantheon in Rome is an empty half-spherical dome 150 Roman feet across, a globe truncated at its equator and set on a high rotunda. The only light comes through a circular oculus 27 feet across set at the pole of the dome, which projects a bright circle of sunlight on the inside of the dome. The circle slowly makes its way around the building as the day wears its course, measuring the progress of the earth around the sun: coffers on the inside of the dome make deep shadows at the edge of the circle that slip perceptibly from one to another. Someone standing in the Pantheon can see the earth move.

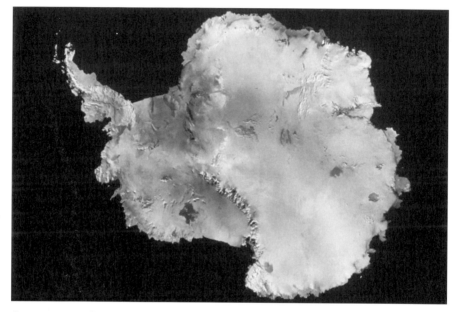

A remote-sensing-satellite mosaic of the Antarctic continent. Courtesy National Remote Sensing Centre/British Antarctic Survey.

3
HOPE

ANTARCTICA

Today's children are growing up into a completely mapped world, which is a new situation. Some important questions remain: where did we come from? Where are we going? How do we cooperate?

HOPE

———— LAND OF THE NOONDAY MOON ————

If you take a basketball-size globe of the earth in one hand
and point with the other at the places where civilization
started, you will see that they are strung out between the
twentieth and fortieth parallels north of the equator, and located on four rivers: the Nile, the Indus, the Euphrates, and
the Huang. It is at these latitudes that humans started plotting
the stars and building monuments and wondering about the
extent of the world. If you hold the globe up in the air and
look underneath, I mean right underneath, where the bottom
pivot of the stand goes in, you will find Antarctica. You will
see that it is tucked away out of sight, isolated by the
Southern Ocean, and all white, covered in ice, as inhospitable to humans as the lands just north of the tropics are
like paradise.

————————

In the Northern Hemisphere June 21 is midsummer's day; in
the southern, it's midwinter's day. The Antarctic Circle—
sixty-six degrees thirty-two minutes south—is where the sun
stays below the horizon on June 21. Three hundred and
twenty miles south of this line toward the pole, the sky is

Icebergs in Antarctica. Photograph by C. Holmes/Royal Geographical Society, London.

dark from the middle of May for two months; at Ross Island, seventy-seven degrees latitude, the same distance again south, and right on the edge of Antarctica, the winter night is three months long. The eight hundred people overwintering on the Antarctic bases—geologists, botanists, ecologists, engineers, cooks—all get up when the alarm goes off at 0730 hours and go about their daily business in spite of the dark. They eat breakfast, lunch, and dinner by artificial light at set times and turn in at 2200 hours every single day. The routine is the way they stay sane. On one of the bases is a group of U.S. Navy volunteers, ordinary sailors, living through the long night as an experiment. Everything is experimental around here. Scientists watch these guys for signs of what they call *over-winter syndrome*. They mean *land of the noonday moon madness:* it's a sort of lethargic claustrophobia similar to suicidal despair.

Thank God they have their dogs with them. Even now that Skidoos and Sno-Cats have made sledge-pulling huskies obsolete, the humans still like to have dogs around. Dogs are good for morale. Huskies are not like other dogs, who watch every movement you make with liquid, loving eyes and make little grunts whenever you go near them. They're fierce beasts, who have to be tethered six feet apart, out of reach of each other's teeth. They eat seal meat and sleep outside curled up in blankets of snow. Perhaps they're good for morale because of their stoical endurance of the elements—or perhaps because it's useful, when overwinter syndrome hits, to have someone you can kick around.

The overwinterers are the most dedicated clock watchers, the most diligent skywatchers, ever. Every day before lights out they pull on their parkas and go out to look at the night. If they're lucky, they'll see auroral storms that fill the upper atmosphere with prismatic colors swirling in double slo-mo, caused by the collision of the solar wind with the earth's own magnetic field. Every night they call up the bases further north, to see how dawn is coming along. When they hear the sun has at last risen two hundred klicks away—a *klick* is a kilometer, in military talk—they rush outside and search for the faint glow of underlit clouds on the horizon, like a distant city lighting the sky with incandescent gas. Up above them, southern star constellations unknown to the ancient Nile Valley astronomers wheel around in tight circles.

When spring arrives in October and the penguins and seals return to breed, the human population of Antarctica swells as well, from its winter eight hundred to about two thousand. The bases are full of new people and bustle. The people stack their crates of stores outside and photograph them, so that when the blizzards come they will be able to find what they want under the snow. They pull on their thermals and their undertrousers and their overtrousers, layer upon layer. These are scientifically improved versions of what the first explorers used to wear, but they look very different. The only clothing they have in common with the heroic age of polar exploration, these new people, is their bearskin mittens. No one wears the beautiful Laplander's shoes that Shackleton's statue on the side of the Royal Geographical Society's building in London has on. He called them *Finneskoe*. They were made of reindeer skin sewn with gut, and the soles were made from reindeer's foreheads—the fur of the reindeer's forehead is the thickest and warmest fur there is. They used to pack these things with dried grass, which absorbed their sweat. To dry the grass, you hold it in the freezing air for a few seconds until the sweat turns to ice, and simply shake it out.

There are about forty bases on Antarctica, from the little encampment of Argentinian families at Esperanza, on the tip of the peninsula closest to Tierra del Fuego, to the thriving U.S. base of McMurdo, just a step away from Captain Scott's hut on the edge of Ross Island. No one clears things away on Antarctica, so Scott's hut has been standing since his disastrous exhibition of 1912 and has now, by default, become a piece of the English heritage.

When Scott lived on Ross Island, the loudest noise was the chattering of the penguins, a sound like a thousand little drummer boys with the flu, gargling and coughing away between drumrolls. In the background there was the thump of 'bergs breaking off the ice shelf and the screeching of the skuas trying to snatch the penguins' babies. Now, all you can hear in McMurdo Base is the sound of the generators. Power for light, power for heat, power to melt the ice for drinking water. So much electrical power is needed to overcome the deep hostility of the environment that throughout the 1960s McMurdo was powered by a small nuclear reactor, like an aircraft carrier. The reactor was not a success. It was removed in 1972 together with fourteen thousand cubic meters of radioactive rock: that's enough to fill the Parthenon.

At the South Pole itself, you will find the silver geodesic dome that covers the Amundsen-Scott base. The pole is marked by a striped barber's pole stuck in the snow, surrounded by the flags of the nations that first signed the Antarctic Treaty. There is an aluminum signpost like the one at the Grand Canyon saying SOUTH POLE in big letters, and a signpost pointing off in all directions with the names of places the current inhabitants come from. It looks like a fun place. People arriving there must think *Hey—it's AntarcticaDisney!*

In the Southern Hemisphere's summer of 1979, November, in New Zealand, a gang of day trippers get on board an Air New Zealand DC-10 and take off for a sight-seeing tour of the South Pole. They are a noisy bunch, well-heeled armchair travelers, Australians, Japanese, and Norwegians mostly, who clink their plastic glasses of Scotch together in internationalist toasts as they cruise south across the Antarctic Circle.

"*Antarctic* is the opposite of *Arctic*," says the flight attendant in charge of commentary for this voyage, "from the Greek *anti,* which means opposite, and *arktos,* meaning bear—and why bear? you may ask."

Well, it is a puzzle, and they do wonder, aloud, noisily, why does *arctic* derive from *arktos the bear*?

"Because the constellation Ursa Major, the Great Bear, appears to skim the Arctic Circle, the line of latitude that marks the line of the midnight sun—and so the opposite, the *Antarctic* Circle, means the southern equivalent."

When the flight ends, the passengers will find out a lot more than why things are named as they are, although there are a lot more names to come. So vastly inhospitable is Antarctica that is has almost nothing human in it, except for the names the first explorers gave to every nook and cranny of the coastline, dedications to their kings and queens, to themselves, to their boats, and to their wives. The flight attendant juggles the ungraspable facts of the ice sheet—as big as all of North America, 40 million years old, the coldest place there is at eighty degrees centigrade below zero—he compares these vast quantities with the little footholds of human experience in Antarctica, "the two-foot-six-inch-high long-tailed red-beaked penguin, Adelie's penguin—a most engaging and inquisitive bird, upon whose oily bodies lost explorers have feasted. They say that penguin meat tastes like chicken stewed in cod liver oil—and that after one month eating nothing but penguin meat you start to dream at night of impossible sugar confections."

It makes a change from the usual in-flight announcements. Here they are, even so, in an airliner, with that gorgeous whistling hum of jet flight in the background, flying at thirty thousand feet over the outliers of the pack ice, and with the first big summer icebergs starting to appear in the ocean below. They peer through the windows to see their first evidence of Antarctica, a flat gray sea full of ice and a horizon ringed with a strange haze. A conjuring line, that horizon, for weird effects of light. As they cross the seventy-fifth parallel, "a line not reached until eighteen forty, right late on, for Antarctica is the last chapter in the book of global exploration," says the flight attendant, the pilot pushes the nose down and they descend to ten thousand feet, so the passengers can get a good view of the smoking crater of Mount Erebus. Antarctica is the most seismically quiet of all the continents, but Mount Erebus still sends up gushes of sulphur occasionally. There is a strange round cloud hovering over the crater, which looks like that thick billow that follows the explosion of an atomic bomb, only whiter and smaller and cleaner. Otherwise the sky is dead blue, and the ice of the Ross Ice Shelf stretches off as far as they can see. Nestling behind Erebus they can see McMurdo Base, a kerosene oasis in the desert of ice, all high-insulation prefabs and four-wheel-drive RVs, looking like some Inuit reservation. Then they are crossing the Queen Maud Mountains, the Antarctic end of the Andes Chain, which push the land up toward them so that they go hurtling low over the ice plateau like a bomber on its final run in, toward the South Pole, three hundred miles away.

"Ladies and gentlemen—the South Pole. This is where the sun in summer transcribes circles in the sky overhead, continuously for months on end. This is where Captain Scott's party lost the race to be first to the pole by thirty-seven days, back in nineteen twelve. They found the Norwegian flag planted by Amundsen and his flying dogsled teams waiting for them"—Norwegian cheers—"and all five of them perished on their way back to base."

The passengers crowd to the airliner's little windows to pop off snapshots of the silver geodesic dome of the Amundsen-Scott base as the plane circles around the pole, banking steeply. They tread on each other's toes and fall into each other's laps, and laugh and cheer. There is a party atmosphere on board as the big plane heads back toward home, their boozy, chatty faces underlit by the sun off the ice below, as though they were flying above the clouds. They go racing back across the mountains and the ice shelf, and the shadow of the plane is as clear as the word *Antarctica* printed in an atlas—and then everything goes white as they fly under a huge bank of cloud. It has whipped up from nowhere, like a blast of trumpets in a symphony, suddenly changing the mood. The uniform whiteness of the sky and the ice merge into one thing, a terrifying maze of clear space. The pilots are taken completely by surprise: in the whiteout they lose all sense of direction. When the Ground Proximity Warning starts to shriek at them that Mount Erebus is rising up right in front of them, it's too late to do anything about it. The plane slams into the mountainside and everyone on board is killed.

The Grim Reaper with his black monk's habit, his skull for a head, and his long-handled scythe seems like an ancient agrarian-age image of people mowed down like ripe corn. It's not, it's an image of Longfellow's, but the Grim Reaper seems as though he comes from the plague years of the fourteenth century, from the time of the Pied Piper. We might be needing him again—who knows what toll future diseases will take?—but we also need a partner for him, who will take care of our contemporary killings, those random, casual, unconnected events that suddenly descend on people out of an apparently safe blue sky: terrorist bombs, armed robbers, serial killers, Legionnaires' disease, and plane crashes, waiting to pick off tourists as they amble about the world lugging their own small world along with them. What shall we call him, this new stochastic image of death? How about the *Grim Sniper*?

I've been a tourist myself. I guess we all have. Scudding over Hudson Bay on the way to Hollywood and Universal Studios, part of the five-mile-high club. Exclaiming at the first sight of the Eiffel Tower, "Ah! Paris!" Perhaps you could even say that contemporary culture is so *universalized* that we are all tourists in our own countries—in our own backyards—moving about our own homes, even, aspirated by prejudice and sentiment—but even so, tourists! Who has any sympathy for them? They don't go looking for experience, they go looking to have their preconceptions confirmed. They go unprepared, because that's the state that prejudice leaves you in. Explorers and adventurers know this and go prepared to be flexible. Military campaigners know it, too, and they go prepared to be stiff, but tourists! They get gunned down by hoods on a Florida freeway and complain that the authorities never told them it was dangerous. They get stranded by floods in Phuket and sue the travel company. They get ambushed in Aswan by fundamentalists with Kalashnikovs, for the part their ancestors played in the subjugation of Islam—well!—where did they think they were, *AfricaDisney*?

Once upon a time, men thought they farmed women. Women were bargained for like plots of land, and the title deeds were transferred from man to man, and the women were used to provide sons. They called it *husbandry*. Virginity was a quality that conferred added value in these arrangements, and because it meant *previously unused,* the term was applied to new land as it was to new women. What a confusion! And we still suffer from it! Not only that—a new confusion has been added to the old. The thought that land development can be damaging instead of beneficial is comparatively recent, and as industry is rapacious, so to be uncultivated is to be virtuous.

I once went to a wedding in a little church in the middle of one of the last forests in England. I had been held up by a major traffic incident, and my journey of two hours had extended itself into four. By the time I got there, the ceremony had started, and I was ushered in silently to a building full of organ music and weeping aunts. The man standing next to me had the leer of a lazy wolf. Gray hair, brown tan, gold cufflinks, white carnation. He winked at me and indicated the bride in her virgin-white clothes with a confidential nod.

"Another butterfly turning into a caterpillar," he whispered. I could smell the fumes of whisky mingling with his aftershave. "The whole thing is back to front. It should be the man dressed in white and supplicating to the female power of the earth. Look at that!" He pointed to the bride's father, whose face seemed to have been clubbed by emotion into solid granite. "Giving her away, he calls it!" he went on, his whisper rising like a sine wave. "He's in the presence of the greatest power he has ever known, his daughter—and he thinks he's giving her away!"

Afterward, as she proceeded out of the church, the bride threw him a big smile, and he caught it with a laugh as loud as the bell of Big Ben. Perhaps that's what she called him.

"Who's using who here, eh?" he said to the whole congregation. "The caterpillar or the butterfly?"

———————

The innocence, the purity, and the paternalism—they are all confusions. What's called virgin land on earth is the culmination of four thousand million years of natural process, vast and implacable. There are huge forces combined in Antarctica, repellent to human life, desperate to deal with. The hydraulic magnitude of the ice and the cold and blizzards to break the body, the perpetual darkness of winter to break the heart. Compared to the subtropical zones in which humans have evolved to live, Antarctica is not an innocent, it's an extreme. In the early years of the twentieth century, as people looked forward to the new age, the newly discovered continent became a trial of hope. One after another, the trading nations of the world sent expeditions down there, as though they were competing to see whose sons could best endure the wrath of this furious virgin. Ernest Shackleton, an Irishman—a Briton, back then—was one of those who went.

When Shackleton's ship *Endurance* was caught in pack ice in the Weddell Sea in January 1915, he and his crew of twenty-seven men spent the whole antarctic winter camped beside it, waiting for it to be freed in the thaw. Instead, they watched

The Scott party at the South Pole with the remains of Amundsen's camp, January 1912. Courtesy Royal Geographical Society, London.

as their ship was crushed to splinters by the huge pressures built up in the shifting floes, and they were marooned, faced with a trek across the disintegrating ice six hundred miles to the nearest land, the remnants of a seal colony called Elephant Island. There were no radios or aircraft then, so the rest of the world was ignorant of their plight. They had to haul two of the ship's boats across the pack ice to get them across the last open-water stretch, hitching rides on ice floes whenever they could, always in peril of gales and of being crushed by the shifting ice, in danger even from killer whales, who can burst up through ice a meter thick to snatch their prey. All through the journey Shackleton shone like hope itself. He made difficult decisions quickly and without equivocation, he sang aloud, he kept his fears to himself. He daily rearranged their little food supplies to eke the last variety from them, knowing that in the extremes of survival, food is a fountain of hope. They reached the island after five months of this existence, their bodies stinking of seal oil, their hair full of ice, their faces baked brick red by the wind: sustained by Shackleton's hope.

Captain Scott is a more famous Antarctic hero than Shackleton. His tragic death on the Ross Ice Shelf is better known than Shackleton's triumph of rescue. The shock of finding that the Norwegians had beaten them to the pole— beaten them *hollow,* in their own humbled opinion—was what killed Scott and his companions. It destroyed their morale. After four months of slogging through the snow, and three-quarters of the way through their journey back to base, Scott and his remaining two companions died in their tent after a week-long blizzard without food or fuel.

Scott left beside his ice-glazed body his diary of their experience, in which he wrote that they had known the risks they took, and if things had come out against them, they had no cause for complaint. At least they had proved that Englishmen could endure. When I first heard this line, I thought it sounded so antiquated and gung-ho. But then I realized their trip was an experiment—and some experiments fail. One generation after the difficult lesson of the Boer War, it was not at all clear whether the British were still capable of proving what they thought was their superior character—and Scott, among others, wanted to show that *one could still do the things he had to do.*

In Trafalgar Square, London, there's a statue remembering Henry Havelock, who was a Victorian hero soldier. The inscription on the plinth bears a date, 1857, and a dedication for the men of his command. "Soldiers!" it says, "Your labours, your privations, your suffering and your valour shall never be forgotten by a grateful country." When I first saw *that,* I had to ask, "And who now remembers what Havelock and his men did?" The first ten people I asked hadn't a clue. It turns out that he was the hero of the Indian Mutiny, who engineered the relief of Lucknow and so helped to continue the British subjugation of India for another ninety years. "And for this he gets a statue?" you might say—but there it is, Havelock had the mettle of an imperial hero, and Scott's question was, Can we still do it? *Is there hope?* And in the amateur-scientist do-it-yourself mode of the time, he set about his experiment.

It is 140 years since Havelock did his deeds, so by the year 2050, the name of Robert Falcon Scott might be forgotten, too. The *Falcon* part is gone already.

There are no Scott-grade heroes in Antarctica now. There are machines to do all that enduring. In fact everything that's done down there, even feeding the dogs, could be done by machines, by remote control. But what point is there in that? We explore because we are humans, so humans have to be there to do it.

"NASA agrees with you," says Shahriar. This is when I first met the man, long before I introduced him to Sally. "People say they have human pilots to facilitate different machine interfaces, but I ask you—if there were no humans in space, what human would vote them funds?"

Shahriar and I met when we shared a summer job at *Popular Geography* magazine. I had joined thinking I would meet people like Livingstone and Stanley, but instead I met Mr. Pursey from accounts and Doris who mops the stairs on Wednesday mornings. My fellow workers turned up holding paper bags with sausage sandwiches in them and described in detail their journeys to work. When Shahriar arrived, it was like fresh air coming in—although he could complain about the rush hour with the best of them. "We are trapped like flies in the hands of a greater power," he used to say. "In fact, I am writing a poem on the subject."

Our job that summer consisted of ghostwriting reports for Antarctic scientists. They used to return from their tours as vacant as midnight parking lots, having spent the past five months watching videos and playing poker and gathering data. We had to take their monochrome and turn it into color for a wider audience. Shahriar was more put out about the lack of human qualities than I was. He used to remind our subjects of the Apollo 13 astronauts—"scientists, just like yourself"—who had to jury-rig their craft and travel back to earth on the Lunar Module's rockets after a technical incident aborted their mission.

"Like Shackleton and his party," I used to add.

"And suppose the astronauts had drifted off into space," says Shahriar, "trapped in the vacuum just as Scott and Wilson and Bower were trapped by the blizzard—who could say they had not been real explorers?"

He was wrong about part of it—the Apollo 13 astronauts were not scientists but air force pilots, following orders—but our men never pointed that out. They sat there in the interview room as dull as glasses of water. It became a sort of game to see if we could spring their personalities from their iced-out brains. Our one success was a Canadian meteorologist called Ted. He had been researching the build-up rate of ice on the Ross Shelf, and the first two days had been a monotonous log of precipitation rates and echo soundings. On the third day we played him a tape of Vaughan Williams's *Sinfonia Antarctica* and cranked up the volume until it was too loud to speak. There is a place in the middle of the third movement, which is called *Landscape,* when the blast of the trumpets changes to a swell of the organ via a shimmer of gongs. It sounds like huge plains of ice and a sky of glowing auroras—did Vaughan Williams visit Antarctica to write it? The change is not a climax, it's a change in dynamics, from one big sound to another. It is amazing what music can do.

"Oh, man!" said Ted when he heard it. "The ice shelf makes noises like that all the time."

"When calving 'bergs?" asked Shahriar.

"All the time, man. You can hear it shifting."

We had made contact. By the end of the session he had told us everything about himself, from a childhood in Saskatchewan skating across ice rinks made by his dad's flooding the lawn with the garden hose, to a stint with the air force releasing weather balloons across the tundra. He had ice in his soul. He told us about the trip south from Wellington, New Zealand, in a ship painted black and blue like a bruise, with an all-Chinese crew.

"They used to go around all the time hugging each other. There were twenty-four of them, and they all looked the same, like twins."

"Duo-dodecatuplets," said Shahriar.

"I don't mean hugging to greet, I mean arms intertwined, like lovers all the time," said Ted.

"Is that what they were? Lovers?"

"I never found out. Everything was a huge joke to them, including the look on my face. They said they were hanging onto each other to keep from falling in the sea. *That Southern Ocean, he's a killer,* they used to say."

Ted told us that he had calculated the current depth of Captain Scott's bones. On the continental plateau, the ice builds up about one inch every year. On the Ross Ice Shelf where Scott died, because it's warmer, the buildup is quicker, something like two feet every year. The ice shelf is itself about the size of France and is the outflow of all the glaciers flowing down from the plateau at longitudes of around 180 degrees. The edge of the shelf is a cliff of ice 700 feet thick, floating on the sea, about 150 feet of it showing above sea level: the breaking up of these edges—there are several shelves, all named after explorers—is where icebergs come from. All this ice, and everything in it, is very slowly moving out from the center. Ted's estimate is that Scott's bones, still within his intact, deep-frozen corpse, are now about 160 feet down and will emerge in the middle of an iceberg in 120 years' time and slowly drift out toward New Zealand.

LAND OF DREAMS

The existence of the invisible Southern Continent was dreamed about and speculated on for centuries before the land was first seen in the 1820s. All that time another land,

Emperor penguins and their chicks. Photograph by C. Johnson/ British Antarctic Survey.

just as unattainable as Antarctica, was clearly visible to everyone: the moon—focus of inspiration and wonder, luminous and mysterious, which, when trodden on, turned out to be covered with a sterile gray dust. It was no surprise to discover that there was nothing on the moon. The surprise came from looking back at the earth. As Shahriar says, *We lost the lover's moon but gained a new beauty.* From the moon, the earth is seen in all its glory, illuminated with color, the clouds swirling around it, life swarming through every minute part of it: the desecrated moon has given us a platform from which to see ourselves more clearly.

If the moon is a platform for contemplating the beautiful world, Antarctica has become a place from which to peruse the changes we are wreaking on it. The heroes have gone and are replaced by scientists, a wonderfully international crew of investigators intent no longer on racing each other to the pole or on naming bits of unnamed land but on unraveling the remaining geophysical mysteries of the earth. The deep ice of the polar plateau accumulates slowly, each year's buildup gradually overlaying and compressing the previous layers. The ice in some places is thousands of feet deep and represents more than a hundred thousand years of buildup. Every year's growth carries with it a trace of the atmospheric gases present at the time. Deep cores have been drilled into these ancient depths, and the analysis shows, from a carbon dioxide level only two-thirds of today's, the last great Ice Age, twenty thousand years ago. There is a greater level of dust present in the depths, too, indicating the furious dry winds that accompanied the glaciation. The ice cores from the end of that period, between sixteen and eleven thousand years ago, show a global warming of around seven degrees, and they also show the rise in carbon dioxide levels for our own little global warming, up from 280 parts per million at the start of the industrial revolution to around 350 now.

———————————

There is a household near me of eight disadvantaged adults whose collective mental age, their psychologists say, is exactly one hundred. They are the sort of people who would have been committed to bedlam in the age of enlightenment but who now live under the care of wardens in ordinary houses. Their experiments in normal life are like a circus act. Every day they make expeditions to the neighborhood shops in little gangs of three or four, sometimes arm in arm, sometimes yelling at each other, always smoking cigarettes. When they pass, they smile enthusiastically if their mood is good, and address the beauty of the day. If their mood is foul, they shuffle quickly past, flashing looks of fear and darkness.

Their warden drives a beet-red Jaguar and looks like he spends most of his time getting his hair cut. He is always on the lookout for people to entertain his little crew. Cake baking, paper folding, performing dogs—"How about slides of Antarctica?" he said to me one day. "They'd love it! I've always thought polar exploration is such a fabulous metaphor for the modern age," he told me. "Such a mysterious place, and hardly anyone's been there. I mean, how do we know it exists? How do we know it's not all a dream?"

Close up, his eyes are as dead as a junky's, which makes his immaculate grooming seem like something dangerous. I think his name is Luther, but he gives the impression that names are superfluous—*just another control trip,* he would probably say. How could I refuse?

"Polar exploration, yes, I could do that."

"Okay! Be there or be square!"

I start the evening with my basketball globe preamble, lifting it up and showing the white continent underneath. "The world is a sphere, like the sun and the moon," I start, expecting to have to explain why all the penguins don't fall off if they're upside down, but no one asks. They are all drinking orange juice, through straws. At the back of the room a large man called Billy with a face as soft as a soap flake sucks his glass dry and keeps on sucking, making the noise that children love so much. Then his friend Benny catches up and joins in. Pretty soon the whole bunch is sucking away in a symphony of rushing air bubbles, until Luther raises his hand and it suddenly stops. Billy and Benny get up and bow, looking like Laurel and Hardy and there is a little round of applause. We turn the lights out and the projector on, and anticipation shifts around the room. The mood is good. My first slide is a twelve-hundred-year-old picture of a monk sailing the ocean in a coracle waterproofed with sheep's wool grease. I tell them it is St. Brendan, looking for the promised land. Slide two is an iceberg.

"This is a column of crystal, as hard as stone, rising from the sea."

Slide three is a whale.

"This is a sea monster spewing out steam."

Slide four is a volcano, erupting.

"This is the firy gate of hell!" I say into the livid darkness. Their innocent faces are lit up by the image of fire as if by fire itself. I am repeating the explanations given by ninth-century chroniclers for what Brendan said he saw when he traveled to the far north. He had been told that the promised land was bathed in perpetual sunlight, streaming from Christ himself. I cannot illustrate the midnight sun with a slide, so I demonstrate it by tilting the globe in the beam from the projector lamp. It works surprisingly well, until a voice comes from the darkness, deep and puzzled.

"Why don't we all fall over in the summer when the earth tilts?" The room fills with a babble of questions that subsides immediately when Luther snaps the light on and glares at them. "Benny! Billy! Shut up!" he yells, and Billy and Benny look as though they've been electrically switched to *hold*. They sit on their hands, hunching their shoulders like enormous children with beards and sweat patches. Luther turns to me again and says, "All yours, professor!"

It's not such a dumb question. Gravity is taken for granted every day, but contemporary explanations of the phenomenon are spiraling into the transcendental. Is it time that is gravity, or gravity that is time? I hold the globe up again and spin it on the tip of my finger, like Magic Johnson. I am not going to attempt an explanation of gravity, but they might just be ready for continental drift. One of the things that children of twelve are encouraged to do at school is to make a paper template of the Atlantic seaboards, the Americas on one side and Europe and Africa on the other, and see how closely they fit together—especially if Greenland is made to fit the wedge at the top.

"The idea of continental drift is that the continents were once continuous with each other, that there was once one huge lump of land that split up and drifted apart under the pressures of the spin of the earth and the convection currents in the hot molten material inside it," I explain. Luther sits watching his petrified charges benignly, while I lecture them.

"The earth's crust is made up of huge plates that are still going through the final stages of this motion, colliding and drifting apart from each other, causing earthquakes and volcanic eruptions all along their edges as they do so. Africa and the Americas are drifting apart, spewing out volcanic material all along the line of the split, down the middle of the Atlantic. On the other side of the world, the Pacific plate is being squashed between the Pacific Rim and North America, threatening to push California down into the magma. India has broken away from the Antarctic plate and drifted north to crash into Asia, crumpling up the Himalayas as it does so. Antarctica itself has slipped right around to the bottom of the globe, out of sight."

They sit there in silence, shuffling their feet. Luther appears to be fast asleep, but then he suddenly says, his eyes still closed, "The story of Brendan reminds me of Atlantis, the lost city of riches out there in the Atlantic." It is as strange as being in the room with a speaking corpse. All the shuffling stops, and all you can hear is the sound of hearts beating. "Perhaps it got swallowed by an Atlantic earthquake," he says.

There is a tiny cough from the center of the room. The smallest woman I have ever seen raises her hand. Her face has the protruding jaw of a Cro-Magnon, and her top lip is covered in down. Her skin is the color of burned wood. "I like the theory that the moon is Atlantis, torn from the earth by some ancient cataclysm," she says, in the thinnest voice I have ever heard. It sounds like the wind whistling through reeds.

It's the kind of story you get from Australia, what they call *Tales of the Dream Time:* How the Kangaroo Got His Tail.

"Is that an aboriginal legend?" I ask her.

"It's a speculation," she says. "What is a dream but questing speculation?" She is perfectly composed. She sits there with her hands folded in her lap as though she's nursing a sleeping pet cat. I look at the others in the room, including Luther, and the more I look the more she seems like the calm eye in the center of an invisible storm. Is it possible to have a mental age of twelve and yet still be advanced for your age?

The Greeks speculated about Atlantis. They also speculated about Antarctica, reasoning that there must be some land down there in the southern Hemisphere to balance the preponderance of the land masses in the north. But what this little tin-voiced woman brought to mind is that there is a parallel voyage in Maori legend to St. Brendan's, and one that took place at around about the same time in human history. A war canoe captained by someone called Ui-Te-Rangiora set out from New Zealand in 675 to travel across the stormy seas between the subtropical and Antarctic convergences—*the Roaring Forties and the Furious Fifties*—until it reached the frozen waters of what is now called the Ross Sea. The next attempt to find the continent came from Captain James Cook, who sailed right around the Southern Ocean in 1773, nosing in and out of the ice trying to find a way through to the south while his countrymen were preparing to slug it out in the American War of Independence. Finally, forty years after Cook, it was the appetite for seal fur, for its luxurious glistening heavy softness, that led humans to Antarctica. It was commercial greed that finally found Antarctica.

The seal traders were followed by the navy men. First it was the Russian Fabian von Bellingshausen who sailed in the Southern Ocean in 1819. The Russian bases on Antarctica today are called after his ships, *Mirny* and *Vostok. Mirny* means peace, and *vostok* means east. The rocket that sent Russian cosmonauts into space was called *Vostok,* too—it is synonymous with exploration for them. East, from where the new day dawns—from where the future comes. In America, the future is in the west—where tomorrow is.

When Captain Ross of the British Navy sailed to Antarctica in the uncharted waters now called the *Ross Sea,* he named everything he saw. He called the first piece of land *Victoria Land,* after the queen. The first island he could land on he called *Possession Island,* after the name of his game.

The second island, on which Scott later built his hut, on *Hut Point,* was called *Ross Island.* The two mountains on it, *Mount Erebus* and *Mount Terror,* are named after the two ships in Ross's expedition.

The French explorer Dumont D'Urville, the man who bought the Venus de Milo to France, sailed to Antactica at the same time as Ross. They were both looking for magnetic south, for magnetism was part of the new science of the nineteenth century. D'Urville named the coast he encountered *Adelie,* after his wife. He named Adelie's penguin after his wife, as well. There were no human aboriginals on Antarctica, but there were plenty of penguins. Adelies are the little red beaked ones with the triangular heads, the only ones that swim with their backs submerged, who live in huge tribes along the coast in summer and who waddle out to investigate each new party of scientists as they arrive. They are as tame as squirrels in the park.

The huge flocks of seals that lived on the islands around Antarctica were also tame. They basked in the peace afforded to animals in a world absent of humans. There were local predators, like the killer whales, but none compared to the sealers who arrived in the 1820s. It was fur seals they were after, and with the fur traders of China prepared to pay good money for every pelt—and for every pair of seal testicles, for Chinese medicine—they wiped out all the seals on each island in turn. When they had pursued the fur seals to the point of extinction, the sealers turned to the elephant seals, not for their skins but for the oil that could be extracted from their blubber. You can still find rusting boilers on the Antarctic islands, which the sealers used to melt down seal oil. For fuel, they used the carcasses of the seals themselves.

When the seals were almost all gone, the sealers became whalers instead, and the specter of extinction widened to include the whales. The quota treaties that the Japanese and Norwegian still balk at are the latest attempt to bring this long period of commercial hunting—a process that has been continuous for five generations—to an end.

Antarctica was dreamed about for centuries and gradually came into clear view on the back of the efforts of the sealers and whalers—so the last slides I show to Luther's over-aged children are of seals and whales and penguins. Sweet seal pups, blubbery elephant seals, and slick black fur seals. The strangest of all is one that eats other seals, the leopard seal. In contrast to most seals, with their deeply communal lives, the leopard seal is a solitary beast. It could be called leopard for its spots alone, but what justifies the name even more is the huge predator's teeth that fill its jaws. When it yawns, it is an appalling mixture of big black baby-eyed seal, all whiskers and cute rolls of fat, and crocodile. When I show the picture, there is a cascade of scared laughter, and someone says it looks just like Benny. Over in the corner, Luther sits with his eyes out on stalks. I think, *It's because it looks just like him.*

When I show a slide of a large flock of penguins standing in the snowy deserts of the Antarctic summer, Billy leaps out of his seat and fetches a children's illustrated Bible from the bookshelf. Amid pandemonium, with Luther shouting and everyone else blinking in the lights he has just snapped on, Billy shows me an illustration of Jesus feeding the five thousand—the miracle of which was not the manufacturing of crumbs into full-blown meals but the persuading of everyone to share their tiny portions alike—and points excitedly at the screen. The penguins do indeed look like the crowd of people in the picture. It's not the cliché of dinner-jacket penguin suits but the way they stand in groups—some close together, some spread out, the way people do—that's so striking. I put my hand up in a dictator's gesture of command, as I have seen Luther do, and the noise subsides. I tell them to turn the lights off again and pretend it is the Antarctic night, and I tell them penguin stories, about how lost explorers have mistaken approaching rescue parties for just another bunch of penguins, and how there are fossil remains on the Antarctic peninsula of giant penguins six feet high, which would have completed the illusion, had there been human eyes in existence to see the sight. And we discuss what the penguins would have said to Jesus if he tried to feed them. Anyone for loaves? "No thanks!" Anyone for fishes? "You bet!"

There is a painting of the early days of science by Joseph Wright of Derby, painted around 1750. It is called *The Air Pump.* The scientist, an amateur, a lover of reason, with long gray hair and a red velvet housecoat, is demonstrating to a small family audience how *nothing can exist in a vacuum.* He has put a parrot into the glass bell of his machine and is pumping all the air out of it, and the bird is suffocating, flapping desperately as its body distorts under the strain of the experiment. Most of the onlookers stand amazed at the dispassionate wonder of the laws of physics, but one—the little girl—is in tears. It is an affecting observation, even though in one of Wright's other paintings, there she is again, torturing her kitten by dressing it in her doll's clothes.

The discovery of Antarctica at the end of the eighteenth century coincided with a new kind of science. Science was no longer to be the study of God's creation—the fish and the fowl—but a study of invisible forces and inhumanly huge time spans: geophysics and evolution. While the sealers were busy hunting on the Antarctic Islands, Charles Darwin was in the Pacific, off the coast of Ecuador in *HMS Beagle,* investigating Galapagos. In Europe, Carl Gauss and Michael Faraday were discovering the relation between electricity and magnetism—and there, suddenly, was Antarctica. A new place, in a critical geophysical position. The pure, uninhabited platform on which the new science might thrive.

The first International Polar Year was held in 1882, the second in 1932. Since then, Antarctica has become a paradigm of international cooperation. There was hope in the search for it, hope in the endurance of its exploration, and now there is hope in the cooperation. The continent is governed by a treaty among twenty-eight states, it is free of wars and murders, it is at peace. Even though the tension between Britain and Argentina simmers across the horizon and the possibilities of exploitation—oil—whales—*krill*—perpetually threaten to engulf the agreement, it is a peace unique in human history. It is not like the peace that prevails by force under empires; nor is it like the precarious peace that exists between angry nations wary of receiving a greater blow than they can give. Nor is it the the expedient peace of adjacent states, biding their time. It is the peace of reason.

————————

The only natives of Antarctica that spend the dark winter on the mainland are the male emperor penguins. The females lay their eggs in April, as the long night is falling, and then leave for the islands. The males tuck the big eggs between their feet and stand there incubating them for two whole months. Their trust in the future is profound. If you are reading this in May or June, think of them down there doing this thing. They are on the coast: behind them stretches a continent the size of Australia, completely covered in ice thousands of feet thick, and all their days are made of moonlight.

II
CHOROGRAPHY

The Great Glen, Scotland, looking south over Loch Oich and
Loch Lochy toward Fort William. Photograph by Patricia and
Angus Macdonald.

4

NATION

SCOTLAND

Your nationality is an idea your ancestors had, invested and reinvested for generations until it seems huge and real. Do you have roots? Are you a tree or a human? Can you carry your nation with you when you go?

NATION

SCOTLAND

―――――――――――― CORPACH ――――――――――――

It is springtime. I am working in a hotel room in Corpach, near Fort William, in Scotland. It is a small room, but there's a large iron bed with sheets as cold and smooth as an ice floe, and a basin in the corner decorated with blue flowers. The rug on the floor looks as though it's been woven from the wool of the local sheep. There is someone else at work in the room. She is wearing a three-piece tweed walking suit, and she has hair cut short and a heavy face. Her eyebrows sit across her forehead in one black swipe. She is poring over a geological map so full of bright colors it looks like a huge exotic, a jungle butterfly, in this dour little room. I have just written what was to have been the first sentence of this essay:

The rocks of the Outer Hebrides, and of the northwest fringe of Scotland, are among the oldest rocks in the world.

"That should be *oldest known*," says my friend, suddenly at my elbow. You should put, 'they are among the oldest *known* rocks in the world.'"

The rocks of the Outer Hebrides represent a time when the continents were still in full drift, two and a half thousand million years ago, and what is now Scotland was well south of the equator. The map of the world looked nothing like it

Ben Nevis from Corpach, Scotland. Photograph by the author.

does now, according to my friend, but what it did look like is open to a great deal of speculation. It is a question of how you interpret the exciting world of paleomagnetic readings, which trace the magnetic orientation of different parts of the earth's crust in Archeozoic times. *Paleo* is the opposite of *neo*. It means *ancient*, and so does *Archeozoic*. By assessing the differences between ancient north and south and present-day north and south, you can make guesses as to where the piece of land in question was before it drifted to where it is now.

"The snag is that paleomagnetic results might imply paleomagnetic longitude, but they do not indicate paleomagnetic latitude!" In other words, you may be able to read old north and south in the magnetism of the rocks, but you don't have old east and west. Never mind, she says, the hunt for oil has thrown up vast piles of new research data. It is advancing what she calls paleogeography in leaps and bounds.

"It's all still so *neo,* we can't stop arguing," she says of herself and her fellow geologists, "especially those Scandinavians." She has glee in her voice. "We love it!" Because a lot of this research funded by the oil industry is going on under the North Sea, Scotland's geology is one of the beneficiaries. She is up here to take advantage of it and to pursue an unlikely thesis that the igneous intrusions of the highland will give a clue to the formations of the clans: this is why we're together. I came up to Scotland to find tartan and thistles and Bonnie Prince Charlie, thinking that that's what highland nationality is, and that it was cradled somehow in the highland landscape, the blue glens of legend. Or is it tartan and bagpipes and whisky? What other nation is characterized so easily by its cultural artifacts? No sooner had I discovered that the situation is more complex—that I was indeed in a vitally national landscape, but that the heather and the shortbread and the Loch Ness monster were not as interesting as what had actually happened—when I met Polly, pursuing her strange notion. I said that looking for clan histories in the rocks underground reminded me of Thomas Pynchon's fantasy in *Gravity's Rainbow* of a bunch of scientists trying to predict the unpredictable fall of V2 rockets over London in 1944. She said well, science often seems strange to amateurs. She showed me a piece of labradorite she had found up in Glen Loy. When I held it, it shone with the colors of motor oil spilled in a roadside puddle.

"Doesn't that look like a rainbow?" she said, and she leaned forward so her face was next to mine, so close I could feel her breath. "And doesn't it look like tartan?" And then it was that she made it clear to me that any study of Scotland has to start with the rocks.

The rocks of Scotland, Polly explained, are not tranquil sedimentary planes. Nor are they the monolithic lumps of stone that young mountains like the Alps are made of. The composition of the ground in Scotland is so ancient, and hence so convoluted and complicated, that the attempt to understand it was what forced the infant science of geology into existence.

"So you see, all this North Sea oil exploration continues a tradition! Scotland has always been the center of geology."

James Hutton's treatise *Theory of the Earth* was the first modern geology. It was published in 1795 and is an account of the principles of erosion, sedimentation, and uplift that Hutton inferred from his observations in the Lammermuirs, the Cheviots, and the Western Isles. It was a comprehensive grounding of knowledge that stood in the face of the catastrophists, who saw geology as the creationists saw evolution: their catastrophe was Noah's flood—*the deluge.*

Radio-isotope dating of rocks is a comparatively recent development. It has given a new thrust to the levels of formal complexity that can be tackled. It also allowed Polly to give me a simple picture of the structure of the highlands. The gneiss of the Hebrides is the edge of the earliest archaic material of the earth's crust, against which the sediments of the ancient oceans, and the volcanic outpourings of five hundred thousand millenniums ago, have been folded and broken and heated and reheated in a mountain maker's kitchen—

and then scoured by the ice sheets into the beautiful peaks and valleys we see today. It is this folded and turbulent material, now cooled to its awe-inspiring steadiness, that makes the highlands of Scotland. Running diagonally across the center, all the way from the Moray Firth in the northeast to Loch Linne in the southwest, is a massive wrench fault known as *Glen Mor*—the Great Glen. At some point in the past—Polly says "three hundred million years BP," *BP* meaning *Before Present,* and about 150 million years after the mountain-building period itself—the two halves of the highlands split along the line of the Great Glen and slid sideways, some say by six or eight miles, some say by several hundred. That's the sort of thing geologists argue about; but slide the highlands did, and indeed they are still tremoring, though so slightly as to be unfelt by us thick-eared humans. Later still, the fault, full of the rubble and the crushed rocks consequent to the *wrench,* was cleared out by the ice sheets and glaciers to make a valley two miles wide and seventy miles long and containing both the famous Loch Ness, the deepest lake in the British Isles, and the famous Ben Nevis, the highest mountain. Because it runs from coast to coast across the center of the highlands, the Great Glen also contains the three English forts erected against the Jacobite rebellions, which were named after the new succession of Protestant kings. The old forts have gone, but the little towns that contained them still remain: Fort William at the southern end, Fort Augustus in the middle, and Fort George at the northern end.

"Don't you love it?" I said. "William, Augustus, and George. I bet there aren't too many highland boys called those names. It's like in the six counties of Northern Ireland—"

"You mean *Ulster*," she said with a sigh. She is impatient with any attribution of historical events to such superficialities as human sentiment. "I know what history is," she says, "I've seen the evidence. History is hundreds of millions of years old. Seventeen forty-five was yesterday!"

Last night I kept her awake with my theory that the whole of Ireland is one. It's obvious if you look at the atlas that all the land from Ballycastle to Baltimore, everything from Malin Head to Mizen Head, must be one, because *Ireland is an island*. Her answer was that if the Giant's Causeway in County Antrim and Fingal's Cave on the Scottish island of Staffa were all part of the same basalt swarm, what difference did nationality make?

"That kind of history is just a jumble of lies told by people with an axe to grind," she said. *Spat*, almost. "We all know about objectivity in the mouths of historians. This attachment they have now to discussions of the lives of ordinary people, to cast an oblique light on the structures of power. God! What an image. It's just like the theater. Realistic effects all done with mirrors. What's so objective about that?"

But this boy's name thing interested me, and I pursued it anyway.

"No—I do *not* mean Ulster, I mean the six counties of the north of Ireland. There are no unionists called James, and there are no nationalists called Billy, all because of the names of the kings at the time of the Battle of the Boyne."

"But that was yesterday," she insisted. "What have you got that isn't passed down the generations by words? Do you know how unreliable that is? It's Chinese whispers! The only real history is millions of years old," she says again, waving her piece of tartan rock under my nose. "And here's the evidence."

I came to Scotland to learn, not to argue: I liked the sound of Polly's paleohistory, and I wanted to hear more. I can see that a basalt pavement that was once a flow of lava but has cooled to a solid is a sort of concrete event, in the way that a building can be seen as a record of the activity of the people who made it. And yes, I was intrigued by the idea that the clans are bound to their own rocks. It sounded aboriginal and crazy and true.

"Okay, Polly," I said. "Tell me about it."

———————

It's only when you see the complications of the rock formations up here that you really begin to comprehend the magnitude of the concrete event. It's prehuman, it ought to be outside our ken, all this boiling volcanic activity. A world of unbearable temperatures, and the sky blocked by sulphur and the earth heaving and throwing out volcanic bombs. The big picture is of these vast continental plates crashing together and squashing the rocks together, but it's the little picture that really illustrates what Polly means. If you can call something as big as Ben Nevis *little*. Corpach, where we are, is right at the southern end of the Great Glen, and we can see the bulk of Ben Nevis out the window. She starts by trying to explain how the mountain was formed.

"The country rock at the time of the Caledonian orogeny was lower- and middle-grade amphibolite schists," she says.

"What?"

"The basic rock was old volcanic material metamorphosed—" she raises her eybrows and I nod, to show yes, I understand that much, "into a harder rock called schist.

There's lots of schist. Lots of different kinds of schist. These around here are basalt, hardened by the pressures of the orogeny."

"Orogeny?"

"Orogeny means mountain building. The one that made the highlands is called the Caledonian, about four hundred and forty million years ago, in the Silurian period." She goes on dropping in definitions as if she is sugaring my tea, one by one until it's sweet enough to understand. "There's a later period of mountain building, originating further west in Germany, called the Hercynian orogeny."

"I see. So there was a Caledonian, a Hercynian—"

"And an Armorican," she laughed. "That's the French one." She collected herself. "Well, not exactly. The Armorican was part of the Hercynian. There was the Alpine orogeny, too, but that was much later. *Anyway,*" opening her eyes wide, to confirm getting back on track, "at the start of the Caledonian orogeny, a massive piece of this schist, a really massive lump, called a pluton, deep underground, dropped down into the molten material of the magma, and the molten material seeped up into the underground cavern vacated by it. When it cools slowly, this stuff, it becomes granite."

"So there was a layer of granite underground?"

"That's right, and then right through the pluton of schist and through the granite layer and all the way to the surface, which incidentally had been overlaid with a fresh flow of unmetamorphosed lava, a split opened up and was filled with different granitic material. The split is what we call a dike."

She looks so serious it makes me laugh.

"What's so funny about *dike*?"

"Nothing at all. Please, continue."

"Okay." There is a pause while she collects herself. "The next thing that happened was that there was another deep-ground subsidence, and a new layer of granite under the old, and then the whole area around collapsed into a subterranean cauldron, but the pluton stayed where it was, sticking out of the ground covered by three layers of granite and with a little piece of lava on top."

"And that's what Ben Nevis is? A volcanic lump stuck onto a granite lump stuck onto a schist lump?"

"Yes, but the point is, there are three different granites exposed, and because they were made under different conditions, their mineralogies are different. And there's still a bit of the original schist in there above the granite and under the lava peak—and on top of all that, the glaciers have scraped and molded the rocks into a different form again. Her face has started to shine with the excitement of communicating these huge and mysterious facts.

"So you see how complicated Ben Nevis is, and that's just one tiny little piece—every mountain in the highlands is different, because of the precise sequence of events, the precise chemical elements in that area, the precise temperatures and folding pressures at that particular location." She is still on her feet, pacing the room, and the quiet dignity of her tweeds framing that eager face makes me want to hug her.

"Sometimes you get a complex happening like this Ben Nevis one, which will then be turned completely upside down and jammed into another location altogether. That's what we call an *intrusion*. You know how every piece of marble is different, because of the swirls and specks of different minerals and rocks that make it? That's the highlands on a huge scale."

I have already seen what she means. Out walking in the glens, you'll come across a crop of rock so variegated that every step you take seems to be over a different type of terrain. You can imagine it coiling and bubbling and moving before settling down and cooling into what you see and touch before you.

"That's what time is," says Polly. "It's what Tom Stoppard says in his play *Arcadia*."

"You mean time is gravity?"

"No! Time is the cooling down of the universe."

I had been planning a walk up the old military road that runs along the Great Glen, but since I met Polly two days ago at the hotel breakfast table and discovered the great world of geology, she has persuaded me to go and look at the Glendessary Intrusion instead. This is a fine example of *early igneous activity in the Caledonides,* just the sort of thing she was attempting to describe. She says it may hold the secret of the clan MacIain. It is a complex of rocks in an envelope about two kilometers by four—the same sort of size as an asteroid — and its cone shape has been inserted into the Glenfinnan schists with its point downward.

"Glenfinnan!" I exclaimed. "That's where Prince Charles raised his standard at the start of the forty-five!" I pulled out my map and discovered that the Glendessary Intrusion is only six miles, as the crow flies, from Glenfinnan itself.

"Six miles on foot, you idiot, and that's over the saddle of *Meall an Tàrmachain,* which is three thousand feet up a forty-degree slope and all the way down again," said Polly. I looked up at her. "It means Ptarmigan Hill. Glendessary to Glenfinnan is forty miles by road. You have to go all the way back down the glen to Fort William and the main road, and then back up Loch Eil, and you have to share the road with all the tourist traffic."

She unfolded a map that showed the site of the Glendessary and several other intrusions up and down the borders of the Great Glen, which it was her project to visit. She showed me a diagram of intense beauty, an apparently abstract construction of enormous detail and complexity, of one of the other intrusions, up behind Dingwall on the Cromarty Firth, which sits on the border between Munro and Ross territory. This is a double complex of foliated granite, which looks in the diagram like an enormous underground peeling artichoke. It was formed at the start of the mountain-building period, but in subsequent cataclysms the granite was recrystallized and then folded repeatedly to the shape it now has, and each of these events brought the formation of a host of new rock types in a huge diversity of proportions and positions. It was all too wonderful; it is true, what she said about the timely diversity of it. I decided that I would follow her to the end of the earth to see this stuff.

"Let's go, idiot," I said to her. "And don't forget to pack your walking boots."

GLENFINNAN

That long day's walk from Glendessary over the top and down to Glenfinnan was the most strenuous thing I've ever done. Polly, too, was drenched in sweat by the time we had clawed our way up to the top, right up into the snowline. At

**The column of the stone highlander at Glenfinnan, Scotland.
Photograph by the author.**

some places it gets so steep that you have to dig your fingers
into the grass and the moss to stop yourself pitching over
backward, and when you do, hundreds of little black spiders
emerge from cover and flee for their lives. Coming down is
just as hard, crossing one leg over the other in splitting
strides with your boots dug in sideways. There is a semicir-
cular concrete railway viaduct at the mouth of the glen, so the
view of the Glenfinnan monument is hidden until it's a mile
away, but when you see it you have to hand it to the old sen-
timentalist who put it up, in 1826. It is a column about thirty
feet high, on top of which is a statue of a man in a kilt and
bonnet, like a small version of Nelson's column in London,
which was erected seventeen years later. Instead of posing
amid a swirl of city traffic, this column stands in the empty

highlands overlooking the beautiful Loch Shiel, as lachry-mose a memory of the failure of the Stuart uprising as the Great Music of the bagpipes or are farewell songs of Robert Burns. It has the oddness of an urban thing in a wilderness landscape, as Polly remarked, "just like Jacobitism itself"— and as she said it, I suddenly remembered something I hadn't remembered for years: playing Alan Breck, the dandy Jacobite hero of *Kidnapped,* in a school play when I was eight years old. My mother made me a gold-trimmed royal-blue frock coat to wear, and flannel breeches to look like moleskin, and a lace cravat at my neck. I even had a sword, hung on stays, and a tricorn hat, and I swear that when I walked on stage the whole audience full of other mothers gasped. An urbane thing—me—in the wilderness—kindergarten.

"That's how Jacobitism became a symbol of freedom," I said. "An urbane thing, liberty, surrounded by the wilderness of English brutality."

There is a spiral stair with a rope banister that winds up the inside of the tower and brings you out at the feet of the stone highlander on top, but we were too late for that, the door was locked. So too was the black iron gate in the little octagonal wall that surrounds the monument, so we had to heave each other over the wall to get close to the tower. The evening was gathering in fast, and the tower felt so remote and unoccu-pied it was as if the clansmen who gathered there to fight for Bonnie Prince Charlie had only just left. It was as though we were the only two in the world. So imagine our surprise to find, on the other side of the tower, hanging on halfway up by his fingertips, a man, with a great bush of dreadlocked hair. When he saw us, he released his grip and jumped down, landing on all fours like a cat. His rock climber's clothes were splashed with Day-Glo and festooned with equipment, and underneath his extraordinary hair, his skin was the color of honey. He was as slim as a macrobiotic chef, and he had the sharpest muscle tone I've ever seen.

"Excuse me, I do not offend, please," he said in a voice that chirruped like a bird. "I am a climber," indicating his ropes and carabiners with a graceful fan of fingers, "from *Romania.*" He smiled the smile of a man in a strange land, like a dog joining a new pack, ingratiating and hopeful.

"Romania!" exclaimed Polly, and her mouth split with the grin of saying the word.

"Isn't the Loch beautiful?" I said. I don't know why, but a riddle came out. "This dark water—it's the depth of the lake coming to the surface to show itself."

"Rubbish!" said Polly, giving me a shove, and she laughed an international laugh at him.

"I am up in the mountains, climbing," he said. "I saw ravens and eagles. I saw a little tiger! Its head was big as a fist!" He held up his fist, and I tried to explain it was *clenched.* Another shove from Polly. Her eyes were twinkling as though she'd found a hunk of treasure in her pudding.

"First things first," she said, and, still grinning, she introduced us and pumped him with little questions and showered him with laughter until he was as relaxed as a native. I had not heard her laugh so much before. She was laughing at things that weren't funny. We found out his name was Pino, his father was Italian, and his Rastafarian hair was not dreadlocked, in fact, but *Moonlocked,* in homage to the British climber Ben Moon.

"I am tomorrow going to Loch Ness. I see a monster, I think?" he said. "But tonight I am looking for haggis and cock-a-leekie." He mimed a man throwing liquor down his throat. "And whisky!"

Well, it was an ordinary ambition: we were in Scotland. Haggis, cock-a-leekie soup, and whisky. We set off together to find some food and drink and a taxi back to Corpach. It was strange to add a third gait to our party. Polly and I had settled to an easy pace together, but Pino was quicker on his feet. He bounced along beside us like a nine-year-old boy. He talked as much as one, too. He was full of the similarities between mountain peoples; that's why he had come to Scotland. He had been to Nepal and Switzerland, and Ethiopia was next. He explained that Romania was a mountain country: "I think you have heard of Transylvania," he said. "You know, the people of mountains are contained by their valleys. Their tribal energy is contained by valleys." This meant, he said, that people in a mountain country can live side by side in peace more easily than flatlanders.

"But the clans in Scotland were forever fighting each other!" I said.

"Excuse me, sir," he grinned, "everyone is always fighting. They fight for fun. But people in valleys know where their land begins and ends. There is nothing to fight about, except if there are too many people."

A very static view of history, I thought. The whole compli-cation of the idea of the nation is that we humans all emerged from one place—Ethiopia?—a hundred thousand years ago, we spread out all over the world, and we've been invading each other's valleys ever since. The valleys may have differentiated us, may have prompted our evolution into different varieties of the same species, even, but that doesn't mean we own them.

"There are no fields in the mountains," continued Pino, on another tack, now. "The mountains are too steep for tractors, so mountain people have cows instead. There are twenty million cows in Ethiopia." He said he once sat down with a calculator and the *Digeste économique du monde,* adding the totals country by country. "One billion, two hundred and nine million, one hundred and seventy-five thousand," he said.

"That's one for every four humans!" said Polly.

"I include also three million buffaloes in the Philippines," said Pino.

It turned out he was climbing the world's mountains on a sort of high-tech rescue mission, free climbing sheer rock faces to remove the bolts an earlier generation of climbers had plugged into the rocks to hold their ropes. He called himself a *deep ecologist* and said that drilling bolts in cliff faces was as bad as building skyscrapers in paradise.

"Too much cultivation?" asked Polly.

"Of course!" he replied. "Like people who take pills to kill bacteria infecting them—what gives them this right? It's white man's medicine." He looked at me—"Excuse me, but I am right. It is only mechanics. Like greenhouse gas emission control: white man's medicine! It is not enough. The only cure for anything is a pure spirit!"

He went on in this vein for a while, as though he thought he could persuade us, and Polly looked as though she was already halfway there. The singsong colorful Pino we had met a few minutes ago had turned into something else, like one of those spiny puffer fish that can inflate themselves to the size of a football. His brow had darkened, and his eyes were glinting with a sinister passion. He started talking about the size of the human population, artificially sustained by industry and agriculture, at great cost to the atmosphere. "Farmers are vicious to nature," he said.

"So how do you maintain the population we have now by hunting and gathering?"

"Not hunting and gathering," said Pino, "just gathering." He had hope for the world. He could imagine it in the future, reforested, peopled by electrically privileged survivors, but by far fewer people than now. He said he had estimated the proper human population of the world by using Belgian statistics of turn-of-the-century Africa.

"The Congo is the size of Europe, had fifteen million people in it in nineteen fourteen. Europe today has three hundred million." He looked at me as if to say, *Are you with us or against us?* and then he said something I remember every time someone starts talking about sustainable development: "We need a reduction in the world's population of ninety-five percent."

Try laughing at that, Polly, I said to myself—and she did. A peal of merriment lofted off her lips and ricocheted off the sides of the glen. Pino stopped walking and held up his hand. "Hear it? That echo! Mountain country! That sound is what I mean!"

Nothing in the highlands is achieved without a bit of a walk first, because the whole region is uncannily empty. So we walked, and got down to describing our different searches, me with my landscapes, Polly with her rocks, Pino with his climbing. We discovered we were all talking about the combination of place and time. I had started with the landscape of the nation being history plus geography—Polly had shown me how enormous the two subjects were, covering the whole universe if you want them to and going back in time to when they started, if you want to go that far—and now Pino showed me how small they were, too. Rock climbing is indeed focused on place and time, but the thrill of it is that it drives out everything else but the precise place your fingertips are lodged and the precise number of seconds your muscles can hold out. The climbers are part of their landscape as completely as those little black spiders in the grass, or the pine martens who slip out of sight into holes in the crags the second they see you coming—*or they could be,* I thought as I watched Pino basking in Polly's fascination, *if they weren't all so narcissistic.*

Just as I was starting to wonder what the Gaelic for third wheel is, we rounded the bend in the road and suddenly there were cars and people and the sound of a highland pipe and accordion band. We crossed over to the building the music was coming from, and the hearty sounds and smells of a dancing party in full swing came gusting out of the door.

"A *ceilidh!*" said Pino, and, turning to Polly, he lifted her hand and danced off into the crowd, boom boom, just like that, and I was left standing alone. It was a joyous swirling chaos, a square room with a stage up at the end all hung with red and green plaids, and four old men were up there punching out the music on drums and fife and accordion and Fender electric bass with enough rhythm between them to sink Trinidad. I made for the dark edge of the room where a row of tables with little white lace cloths made havens for

sweaty, cheerful kilted men and women in gowns to sit out
the dances they couldn't keep up with. I could see Pino and
Polly whirling around in a group of four, and I sat down at
the nearest empty seat to figure out my next move. I didn't
have to wait long. From the darkened corner of the table I had
chosen came a voice, duff and sour.

"*Cnuic 'is uillt 'is Ailpeinich,*" it hissed, and I turned to
find an old man in a blue blazer and a white linen shirt showing the creases of clumsy ironing along the collar. He was
glaring at the dancers—his *cnuic 'is uillt 'is Ailpeinich* was a
little curse for them, nothing to do with me. He turned his
head and looked straight at me and spat out a translation. His
head was sunk down right into his shoulders, like a granite
pluton sinking into the magma below.

"Hills and rills and Alpines, always," he said.

"Excuse me?" I said.

"All this—*claptrap,*" he said, spreading his arm around
the room, at the tartan swags and the bagpipes and the tots of
whisky and the whole kilted, sporraned throng. "All this
came in with the damned Germans." He spat on the floor.

"Excuse me?" It was hard to hear above the music.

"And why should I do that, young man?" he said. "I'm
speaking the truth, and I'm speaking it as a MacAlpine, and
the Alpine became the first king of Scotland one thousand
one hundred and sixty years ago."

"So you mean the Saxons?" I yelled at him.

"I mean the Germans! The Hanovers!" He waved with dis-
gust at the dancers. "Those are not kilts, they're fancy-dress
costumes! That's not tartan, that's pretty patterns! These are
not highlanders, and they're not dancing highland dances,
it's only party games!" At this moment Polly and Pino came

into view—neither of them born anywhere near a glen, just as the old man said. They were whirling around and around in a lovely imitation of a highland reel, Pino with his sinewy thinness and Polly with her thickset jaw, both laughing their heads off with the joy of it. My companion saw me looking at them, and the lump in my throat must have been visible.

"Your manly lass, with her manly African, just look at him! He has arms like Rob Roy MacGregor!" Rob Roy had arms so long he could pull a dirk from his sock without bending his back.

"He's a climber," I shouted. "I bet you didn't know climbers can dance!"

"Oh, he can dance for all that," said the old man. "The old highlanders danced in squares on the beaches, before the boats that took them to America. The dance started slow and mournful, and full of tears of farewell, and got faster and faster until the whole boatload was swinging each other around in a frenzy. It was not so much a joyous thing back then."

"Square dancing is what it's called in England."

"Aye—in English. Trust them to see the soldiery in it. The English always were a people for putting things in their place." He spat on the floor again.

Everyone knows that the French are libertarian and posturing and that Persians are proud and that Norwegians are earth-solemn and that the Russians burst into tears at the drop of a hat, and the English are stuck to class like men electrocuting themselves on a four-hundred-volt cable—but is that what a people is? Everyone knows that a nation is held together by its money and its language and its laws—but what has the land they live on got to do with it? The highlanders were the last tribal people in Europe, living as close to the land as you can get—that's why the highlands are a suitable subject for someone looking into a national landscape. It is more complicated than the crystalline structure of plagioclase, as beautiful as that is. I thought I'd leave the rocks alone for a bit and look at the history after all. I could let Polly and Pino get on with it and talk to this old man instead about what had happened to Scotland.

"Whisky for you, sir?" I said. His hand crept across the table. "Alistair MacAlpine," he said, as I shook it. "And it's gin for me, sir!"

Old, lonely Mr. MacAlpine, his tongue loosened by my companionship as much as by the drinks I was buying him, told me everything. He had the whole story of Prince Charlie Edward Stuart's doomed escapade: from the night before Glenfinnan spent in MacIain's house up in Glen Alladale, through the victories at Prestonpans and Falkirk and the sacking of Forts George and Augustus, to the desperate calamity of the battle of Culloden, and Prince Charlie's escape back to France assisted by Flora Macdonald—"A woman of rock," he said, "A woman of gold." After the battle the duke of Argyll—"The tool of the English who fought on the English side at Culloden, *the traitor*"—gathered up the swords of the dead highlanders on the battlefield and used them to make railings for his London house. "And he was but the first of many traitors. Those who came next were worse still, because they betrayed their own children."

After Culloden the duke of Cumberland, son of King George, commander of the English forces, took about the suppression of the highland clans with such brutality he was known as *Butcher*. His real name was William Augustus.

"What does it matter what you call an English king?" said MacAlpine, and he broke into song, which set his old jowls quivering for two short lines: "*We're bought and sold for English gold—such a parcel of rogues in a nation!*—Ah! Man! Boy! It's too late now, too late!"

He slumped back into his chair, and although I was impatient to hear about the clans, I could see that I was in the presence of an authentic highland lament for lost land, so I sat silently.

The dance band were taking a rest, and the tables filled up with swarms of dancers, descending like a flock of birds on new pasture. Polly and Pino came and thumped down at the table and sat panting and red in the face with soaking wet hair. MacAlpine looked up and said to Pino, "You look like a couple of race horses after the chase, young man. Take your lady and walk around to cool down, and have something to drink."

"Take a horse to the water, but you cannot make him drink!" said Pino. Polly thumped him on the arm—"I'm not a bloody horse"—and yanked him to his feet, and they went off toward the buffet.

"That's got rid of them!" said MacAlpine. "Now, you want to know about the clans," and just as he'd rattled about Bonnie Prince Charlie, off he rattled again, the tears that had appeared when he broke into song still glistening on his cheeks.

The word *clan* in Gaelic means children. The chief was the father of his clan: he was bound by that to them as they were to him. Democracy would have meant nothing to them. "A clan with an elected chief would be an orphanage, not a family!" The clan-families lived on family land, in a feudal state of reference to the chief, and MacAlpine insisted that I should understand this point, that *feudal* does not mean hopelessly medieval; *feudal* means *family.*

"Your children in their rooms that they keep in a fine mess, and expect you to knock on the door of, and keep out of in your own house—is that not a feudal arrangement? The responsibilities of a father are as deep as loch water. They mirror the man's authority as the lochs mirror the mountains."

I thought back to the family I had left behind me in the south. Authority? Feudalism? Living in my house is as argumentative as living in the House of Commons. "And are the women not to have authority in the clan?" I said.

"The women do the work, while the men get on with fighting the men of the clan in the next glen," he said, and the first smile I had seen on his face appeared. "And do you know why the inheritance has come to pass through male lines? I'll tell you—it's because no woman can live in peace in her own mother's house!" He laughed and slapped my back and took another gulp of gin and slammed his glass on the table. Little drops of spittle were clinging to his lips.

He went on to the betrayal by the highland chiefs after Culloden, when the English forcibly removed their paternal powers and forbade them to carry arms or to wear their clan costume. Within a generation the blood tie of feudalism had been replaced by the market forces of the new agriculture, and the chiefs had racked the rents of their land to a point where the people of the clans could be evicted for nonpayment. This is what they call the Clearances: the people were moved out of the highlands by force, and the land was turned over to sheep grazing—and when that market slumped, the whole of the Caledonian orogeny lay as empty and desolate as it still does today. You might find such colossal emptiness beautiful, as you speed down empty roads past towns consisting of five houses, four of which are hotels—but poor old MacAlpine felt the injustice as keenly as if it had happened before his own eyes. It happens all over the world, this carrying forward of ancient grudge from generation to generation. It's the twin of heritage, handed to become sinister, and both of them cling to nationality like second skins. We evoke old times at our peril.

I love the way time is embedded in the world. I love the way you can look at mountains and see them in the instant of the present, and know that they've been as they are now, this instant, for hundreds of thousands of years. I love the time of history, too—I have a bent for chronology. I think that the chronology of a place is as coordinating as its map coordinates. So I asked him when all this had taken place.

"You want an example: I'll give you that of the MacIntyres who held Glen Noe from Campbell of Breadalbane, and who had paid a rent of one snowball and one fatted white calf for centuries, until the rent became money, and the worst happened. They were evicted and sailed for Canada in eighteen hundred and six." So, I said, the Clearances took place at the same time as the enclosures in England, and at the time of Napoleon, when the whole of the rest of Europe was on the move—and my mention of this coincidence suddenly sent the old man off on another tack.

"The pipe-clayed gaiters of the Black Watch are there to re-mind the men of the rags their forerunners wrapped around their bleeding feet on the retreat from Corunna!" he said, and because he had now drunk enough gin to make him fierce and had struggled to his feet and was standing and swaying from side to side, and because the dancing had started again and Pino and Polly were locked in an embrace at the far end of the room, I decided to leave the whole business behind me and get on up to Fort Augustus and think about it all. I stepped out into the Highland spring twilight and hitched a ride along the side of Loch Eil back to Fort William, and then went by taxi another twenty-five miles up the Great Glen to Fort Augustus: the town from which, I could not help think-ing as I slipped into sleep in my little hotel bed, Butcher Cumberland had sent out death squads to hunt for rebels and kill their cattle and burn their houses and rape their women.

─────────────── CREAG NAN CLAG ───────────────

I was visited by a ghost that night. It was unpleasant. When people say they've seen a ghost, I now think, *You can't have!* You don't *see* a ghost, you *feel* it. It's like having a beast in-side you slithering around your thoughts. It's like living two lives at once. Everything is speeded up. Your heart beats twice as fast, and sweat oozes out of you like juice out of a fruit press, although you don't realize that until the ghost leaves, which it does as suddenly as a light switched off, and then you find yourself as wet as if you'd run ten miles, but shivering cold, without the heat of the exercise.

The author on the summit of Creag Nan Clag, Scotland. Photograph by John Shepheard

I don't know who the ghost was. It settled on the carpet as light as a spider, and I sat bolt upright with my heart choking me, oozing sweat, and with what felt like a pair of hands grasping my brain. I was helpless, jammed fast with the speed of my pulse and with these careering sensations in my brain. In the end, it was benevolent, it was showing me something— but I hate to think what a malicious haunting would be like. People are turned mad by bad spirits. Their hair turns white and they never speak again, for fear of alerting the ghost.

What my ghost showed me was the formation of the highlands. There were the rocks bubbling out of the magma and
crystallizing in millions of shards of color, bright interference
colors like the blue on a butterfly's wings, and the colorful
smudge of rainbows. There was the whole highland landscape coming into being. I couldn't see it; I could feel it. The
whole landscape, from the plain of the Forth and Strathmore
out as far as the Western Isles, was bubbling and foaming like
a sauce on a stove. There were the Etive and the Nevis masses
pushing out of the cauldron, and the waves of folding rock
crashing against the shield of Moine. Mine wasn't the view of
a space shuttle pilot, pressing his Hasselblad against the window—I was down there among it, even though I could comprehend it all. I watched while it all stabilized to a crust, and
then there was a massive wrench as the Great Glen slid apart,
the sea in the Moray Firth bubbling and writhing in the cataclysm. Then I became aware of bodies filling the glen, like a
painter's vision, thousands of humans all chattering in their
secret tongue of Gaelic, and I realized that this was the rebellion, this wrench, and when the ice came grinding through
and cleared out the glens and overlaid the land with freezing white, I felt it was the coming of the English, and the
Clearances, and the ending of the way things were. Just as the
ice was melting, leaving behind it the way things are, I was
released from the grip of the haunting, left soaking wet, sitting up in bed, staring at the mirror of the hotel dresser in the
corner of the room. I staggered over to the window and flung
it open to a pure moonlit night, and the steady summits of the
side of the glen and the smooth water of the loch looked just
like what they were.

I don't know whether a haunting takes something away from you or puts something in. It was as though all the background had been cleared away. I now had a strong desire to walk up the length of the Great Glen. I would go all along the side of Loch Ness on the old Hanoverian military road to Inverness, which stands where the glen runs out into the sea. *Inver* means *mouth*.

I had a goose egg breakfast, poached on toast, and the huge pale yolks tasted like fuel for a fighting man. I pulled on my boots, packed my rucksack, threw my map case around my neck, grabbed camera, binoculars, and compass, and stepped out on the road. I passed by the Benedictine abbey, which now stands like a huge granite confessional on the site of Butcher Cumberland's fort. A half mile out of the town, as I came to the center of the glen floor, a deer leaped over the wall on one side of the road, took a couple of bounds in front of me, gathered itself, and leaped over the fence on the other side and ran off across the fields with its white ass looking like a flag against the grass. Loch Ness fills the glen from here all the way to Inverness, twenty-six miles, and the hills on either side rise up at forty degrees to around fifteen hundred feet. The loch is the biggest body of water in the highlands, not because it's wide but because it's deep, and it has the character of an inland sea. Depending on the brightness of the sky, which it reflects, and the state of the wind, which disturbs the reflection, it can be gray with white waves or as smooth as glass, taking on the color of the oaks and beeches on the sides of the hills. Today the whole expanse glowed blue like pale gunmetal. I walked on up the road, which climbs up the side of the hills on the south of the glen before coming down again to run along the shoreline after the waterfall at Foyers. I had climbed a couple of hundred feet when suddenly two pale gray interceptors from the air force base at Lossiemouth came barreling along the glen, so close to the water that they were below me. The sides of the glen are about a mile apart just there, and the thunderous sound of the jets cannoned off them and filled me with elation. I could hear the whole glen, and I saw it all, too, in that one moment, and I could understand how the steep-sided glens were home, and the clans were families living in them, and how the Great Glen runs down the middle of the highlands and collects the other glens up, and makes them one nation.

National is a dirty word. The colonialist Europeans—none more than the British, including plenty of Scots—made it dirty. Hitler made it dirty, and his imitators make it dirty still. When I mention the idea of a national landscape to my friends, most of them shudder in case they should be seen even thinking about such a thing. *National* means military might. It means dictators and the abuse of power. It means xenophobia. It means being little, and not of the great world. Nationalism seems to confuse ethnicity with territory the way ethnicity confuses race with culture: everything is pre-destined. But who denies that the geography of the land they inhabit holds people together and makes them what they are? You can stand on the marshy flatlands of West Friesland, or East Anglia, under the huge sky, whose light fills lowland painting with such minute detail, and you can feel, like the people who live there, that there is no place to run to, no place to hide. This is where Puritans come from. Or you can stand in the up-and-down country of Wales and sing to the mountains and listen to the echo coming back, and feel as clever and emotional as a Welshman. You can roll across the steppes of Eastern Russia on a horse, galloping, and realize that with a few thousand others, with momentum like that, you could conquer the world, as the Mongols did. That's how I could stand in the glen-furrowed world of the highlands and see in them a land of families, linked together by *feud*— in all the senses of that ancient and mysterious word.

Homo sapiens is currently reckoned to have sprung out of a primate mutation in the African rift valley. I like the idea that the species evolved in the fringe of the ocean, where we went to escape the great drought that afflicted the earth ten million years ago—it's why people like mucking about on beaches. Our upright posture is really a swimmer's horizontal. Spending most of the day in water to keep cool, we lost our hair and developed our voices, as the dolphins did; we developed genitals appropriate to underwater mating, face to face, as the whales did; but unlike them, we came back on land when the climate improved for us, and we started to spread out from East Africa to cover the globe.

None of this is a recipe for *homeland*. The Australian aborigines maintain a clan system that is nomadic, spread out over the whole continent. The mnemonic litany that keeps the memory of the clan alive is called a *songline:* it is tacked down by pieces of landscape but not located in any one place. Neither is there a homeland implicit in the political idea of *nation*. Millions of individuals are arranged for matters of convenience into nations, in which language, law, and money stand as the qualities of nationhood. This is not so much a collection of nations as a collection of currency zones, rubbing along together. Added to this, all through the density of nationally located cultures are the diasporas of people who live in landless zones of language and custom. The peoples of the world remind me of the continental plates—having drifted slowly into position, we are now fixed by the ethnic equivalent of cooling—the pressure of the weight of numbers of other people. There is friction at the edges, at the equivalent of earthquake zones. The Balkans have been just such a juncture for centuries: between Islam and Christianity, between Slav and Hapsburg, between Russia and Europe, between Moscow and Washington. They are a sort of topological pivot, like the whorl of fur in a dog's coat, where all the different naps of growth coincide in a furrow on its chest. Afghanistan is another: people can't sit still in these places, and they never will.

I had walked and walked while turning this subject over in my mind, up the road built by English soldiers after the first Jacobite rebellion—Charlie's father's—in 1715. The idea was to bring control to the region by establishing garrisons along the Great Glen—Fort William, Fort Augustus, and Fort George—and to connect them by roads so the army could move swiftly between each one. The road I was on was the first to run between Fort Augustus and Inverness. It is easy now to leave the road at any point and plunge off into the heath and heather of wild country, into the *forest,* as it was then called. It is not until struggling over rough ground, over the boulders, through the heather and bogs, that you realize the strenuousness of highland life in the clan days. You can see why a man wears a kilt, to cope with the mud on his legs and the sweat on his body. Out in the rough country, it is easier to understand the unusual classlessness that went along with old pride in name and rank. People who live strenuous lives value strength above everything.

At its summit, before it starts downhill again to run alongside Loch Ness, the road passes by the plug of an old volcano called *Creag nan Clag*—Bell Rock. It pushes out of the ground smooth and fissureless, like the stem of a great plant, and rises to fifteen hundred feet—but you can scramble up its back, where heather grows on material left behind by the ice sheet moving northwest, and look from the top out toward Inverness, ten miles away, and see the bridge across the Moray Firth and the snowy bulk of Ben Wythis, another five miles on. The great mountain is so bullishly white with snow, it looks like a cloud on the horizon against the blue sky, hovering over the huge empty waste of the highlands.

It was up on this summit of Creag nan Clag that I had my last encounter in the highlands. When I think about him now, I call him *the last of the MacGillivrays* because of the subject he brought up. I had found a summit rock, clear of vegetation, right at the edge of the cliff that plunged down hundreds of feet to the shores of Loch Ruthven, and I was sitting on it, cooling off the exertion of the climb, eating chocolate. I had in me the mixed emotions of the uplift of the highlands and the melancholy of their desertification. From my aerie at the top of the mountain, I saw the last of the MacGillivrays and his little red dog making their way on the road far below me. I sat and mused on emptiness while the two of them climbed steadily up toward me, now and then disappearing from view behind a heathered headland or an outcrop of rock, and then reemerging looking a little larger, he plodding steadily, the dog darting about like a minnow. It was some ferocious little snapper of a terrier, and when I looked through my binoculars I could see its mouth open and shut, and then hear its yelps as they came up to me, delayed by the distance. They were at that point crossing a field fenced off from the rest of the hill, containing half a dozen long-haired cows and their calves. The little dog was trying to face down one of the cows, who was anxiously, and with some verve, trying to reach her calf, which was standing dumbly on the wrong side of the dog. The man was already carrying a burden on his back, as big as a bag of fardels, but he swept the little dog into his arms and plodded on up the hill, clutching it to his chest while it finished its argument with the cow, barking its stupid head off. Then they disappeared again for some time, and when I next saw them they had come right into hailing distance and were making straight for my summit, the dog restored to the ground and leaping from rock to rock so as not to scrape its belly on the heather.

The bundle the man was carrying turned out to be a parachute, the kind you can sit in and steer, and we talked while he got it ready. He laid it out on the ground like a kite, and it was big: it covered the plot a house would have. He strapped himself into a harness and connected it to the shrouds of the parachute, which stretched out behind him across the ground like the train of a wedding dress.

I told him I was bound for Inverness, and then on up to Culloden Field and Fort George.

"Ah, Fort George, that's a grand place. It's built out of red stone, and the air's so clean up here it's still as red as the day it was made."

"The color of blood?" I said, thinking, *How appropriate for a fort.*

"Well, no," he said. "It's pale. It's the color of offal. Guts." He was about thirty years old, with a banker's haircut and a sporty tan. He spoke as if he were practicing for leadership. His voice was modern Scots—bleached out by television studio lights, perhaps. "It's one of the forts the English built to reinforce their brilliant idea for getting rich. Colonialism." He said that colonialism was born out of the island life, a not uncommon notion, but he had his own word for what Britain now was: he called it *discontinental.*

"Do you know Fort William?" he asked, and without giving me time to answer, "There's another Fort William in Calcutta. First garrison of the East India Company. It's where the Black Hole of Calcutta was do you know the story?"

"No," I said.

"Look it up when you get home." I did: The Black Hole of Calcutta was a punishment cell on the parade ground at Fort William, which heated up in the Indian sun like an oven. It was where they put *refracted* soldiers in solitary confinement. When the fort was overrun by the Indian prince Suraju'ddaula, with French help, he declared the cell the only piece of territory the British could lay claim to in all of India, and he repatriated all 146 survivors of the garrison into this tiny brick hut and left them to die; as they did, they remained standing upright, wedged in by the bodies of their compatriots.

"That was in seventeen fifty-five. It was what Clive of India went out to avenge, and he ended up with the English owning the whole of India. There's another Fort George, too, in Canada, Hudson Bay territory, from the wars with the French at about the same time over there, Wolfe, Quebec, that one; did you know Wolfe commanded a battalion at Culloden?"

"No," I said.

"And of course there's a Fort William Henry in the *Last of the Mohicans,*" he said with a smile. "Same wars, further south, on Lake George—another George!—on the New York–Vermont border. Delaware country, according to Cooper."

By now he had strapped his helmet on and looked as though he was ready to jump, and although I can't say I enjoyed his conversational style, I was suddenly spurred by this thought of the North American Indian nation, and I didn't want him to leave just yet.

"Are you a native of this country?" I said.

"My mother's name was MacGillivray," he said. "They were part of Clan Chattan. That was a confederation of small clans. Means Clan of the Cats. MacGillivray led the charge at Culloden," he said, matter-of-factly, not puffed up with tears and pride as old MacAlpine would have been. He pointed out to the west. "The clan duthus was Strath Nairn, just the other side of that ridge, but it all broke up in the eighteen fifties."

"What's a strath?

"A river."

"What's a duthus?"

"Gaelic word for hearth. Means the clan center. Whoever first lit a fire on a piece of land and sustained it long enough to boil a kettle of water owned the land."

"But you don't live there anymore?"

"I said already. It broke up in the eighteen fifties." He flashed a big white grin at me. "I live in Edinburgh. Nightlife's better."

The 1850s: about the same time as the North American Indian wars of longitude 100 degrees west. I could imagine some MacGillivray, forced to emigrate to America, staking a claim in Wisconsin and pushing the Dakota off his land by force, and I attempted to raise the irony of this—but irony is lost on such people. He deflected it as men born to lead do, with cheek:

"What goes around comes around," he said. And then: "Come on, Augustus," and he picked up his dog and nuzzled its fur with his nose, stuffed it into the harness, picked up the shrouds of his parachute, and ran straight off the edge of the cliff, leaving me standing there while they flew off down the valley. This is what leadership is. You talk knowledge, mention your mother's pedigree, kiss the dog, and jump off a cliff. *Don't let the bastards interrupt your stride.* I was impressed.

And I was cheered up. I felt the haunting and the melancholy go from me as Augustus's frantic yelping disappeared into the huge silence of the hills. Scotland is a beautiful place, full of colorful stories of strife and passion. There is enough meat on the hoof, enough wood in the forests, and enough hydroelectricity in the glens to have a life as richly familial as the people who lived there before. The whole thing could start again. There are about five million Scots, of whom four million live in the four thousand square miles of the lowlands, and three million of them in the cities. The other million live in the twenty thousand square miles of the highlands. There are more people in the highlands now than there were before the Clearances, but what is just as important is that there are more Scots in Canada and Australia and the United States than there are in Scotland.

From where I stood, looking over the highland landscape, it was clear that the geography of the glens reinforced the custom of the duthus. I concluded that that's what a national landscape is. You move into a place, and after a few generations it has changed you, and you have wrought your culture, using the landscape as an anvil. But nothing lasts forever. If you are evicted from this landscape, the first thing you might do is to get drawn into the cycle of revenge. Another thing you might be able to do is to start again—and is that not what the national idea of the United States was? Or you can depend on your memory, as a nomad has to do. The tartan, the bagpipes, and the whisky are like the songlines of the highlanders, even if, when you look closely, you can see the fingerprints of the marketing people. The colors of the vegetation, the sound of the mountains, the taste of the water—that's what tartan, bagpipes, and whisky are. They are the landscape now: and in the beginning, we are all nomads.

The Netherlands from the space shuttle *Challenger*, November 1985. The Zuyder Zee is between the clouds at the bottom of the picture; the Rhine Delta is at the top. Courtesy National Aeronautics and Space Administration.

5
UTILITY

F L E V O L A N D

Turning the land to profit has been the underlying strategy of moves in the landscape for so long it is easy to forget how beautiful utility can be. Is it still possible to think of the greatest possible happiness for the greatest number of people?

UTILITY

――――――――――――――― AMSTERDAM ―――――――――――――

The big North Sea storms are most prolific at the beginning
and end of the winter. This is when the equinoctial tilt of the
earth moves the conflict between the low-pressure air
masses of the North Atlantic and the high pressures of the
mid-Atlantic over the British Isles and the lowlands.
Turbulent frontal weather systems arise out of this conflict
and drag gale-force northerlies down from the pole toward
the English Channel. Every so often these winter depressions
accumulate such a steep rake that the pressure is rising at a
rate of one millibar every ten miles, and that's when you get
hurricane-force winds howling south, pushing water before
them into the narrowing basin of the southern North Sea.
Should such an event coincide with an exceptionally high
tide, when the moon is pulling the sea level up by a few feet
above usual, the combined effect of wind and tide can cause
big floods in the lowlands. Sea water rushes across the flatland, drowning cows and sheep and depositing them in the
treetops, swamping houses and sending streams of refugees
to higher ground.

In Holland, in earlier times, these floods were given the
name of the saint's day in which they came, as though heaven
were implicated, rather than the movement of planets. There
is the *St. Elizabethsvloed* of 19 November 1421 and the

The observation tower on the Afsluitdijk, the Netherlands, looking northeast. J. W. Cronijn—Kiosk Monument Afsluitdijk.

St. Pietersvloed of 5 March 1651. On All Saints' Day 1570 there was the *Allerheiligenvloed.* The most recent occurrence was in 1953, when the sea defenses were breached on both sides of the North Sea, and people in Felixtowe and Walcheren and Canvey Island and Middelburg woke up to find a nightmare, with the external world freely flowing through the internal, their staircases descending into cold gray water. It was the night of the 1 February: it should be called *St. Bridgetsvloed.*

On the day I traveled to the Netherlands by boat, it was midsummer, and the sea was as calm as a duck pond. I was on my way to a conference in Amsterdam with the theme of machines in the landscape, to which I was contributing a seminar on experimental landscapes. My research was all founded on the Pamlico Sound, North Carolina, and the sand spit where the Wright Brothers first flew. The spit is formed by the Gulf Stream traveling north and the Labrador Current coming south. At Cape Hatteras, thirty miles south of Kitty Hawk, you can see where they meet, drawing the sand out into an arrowhead. You can splash in warm water on the south side and cross the sandbar a short way and splash in cold water on the north side. A constant wind comes off the Atlantic at twenty-five knots, and this is what bought the Wright Brothers and their gliders there. That, and the presence of sand dunes to elevate their takeoffs and cushion their crash landings. Behind the sand spit on the lagoon of Pamlico Sound is the site of an earlier experiment, Roanoke Island. It was there, three hundred years before the Wright Brothers, that Sir Walter Raleigh set up his first New World colony. At the conference I would describe the area as a frontier of experimental landscape strategy.

I went by boat so I could take my bicycle and travel east after the conference to visit the polders, the lands the Dutch have reclaimed from the sea. My bike is a Taiwanese thoroughbred, but its colorful line was submerged beneath eight pannier bags, which kept me in low gears the whole time I was in Holland. Millions of people ride bicycles in Holland, even though the whole country is flat and windswept and tough to pedal in. When I crossed the big barrier dike that runs across the top of the Zuyder Zee and governs water levels in the interior, I was lucky enough to have the wind behind me. The dike runs twenty miles across the open sea in a dead straight line. At the halfway point, I met a group cycling the other way, straight into a headwind so strong it made their clothes flap like rags.

They were exhausted. They looked like the retreat from Stalingrad.

The polders are the ultimate product of centuries of Dutch hydraulic practice. Necessity has driven the Dutch to become the masters of sea defense: 65 percent of the Netherlands is liable to inundation even from regular tides. Although the North Sea coast is protected by huge ranges of sand dunes, there were two ways the sea could get in, now both secured by long barrier dikes. The first was the Rhine-Scheldt delta south of Rotterdam, and the second was the Zuyder Zee, which filled the center of the country, a sea some thirty miles wide and sixty miles from north to south. The barrier dikes keep the sea tides out—and they also make huge freshwater lakes, which are filled up continuously by the rivers of the Rhineland. So, the Zuyder Zee is now the IJsselmeer, part of whose shallow bed has been further ringed with dikes and drained, producing four polders about fifteen miles square. They are flat landscapes of vast fields gridded with hundred-acre farms and dotted with brand-new settlements. Modern places—twentieth-century landscapes—where utility has been encouraged to flower. If the *Utilitarian Landscape* suggests to you a place of industry and intensive farming, big roads and pylons under smoke-filled skies, go and see the polders. All those things are there, but it feels different—it feels like recreation.

I first went to the polders as a boy, in 1960, and saw them half built and still under their first crop of reeds. My father had a birdwatching streak, and he had taken me to see the spoonbills and marsh harriers that were taking advantage of the new land. I was twelve and had my own agenda to think about, so on the long drive I got him to recount the entire history of World War II. I wanted to know all about Rommel and the Battle of the Bulge, and radar and Omaha Beach. One of the things he told me about was a cordite factory he had worked at in Wales, which consisted of eight hundred separate buildings, most of them house-sized wooden sheds separated from each other by earth mounds as high as the roofs, in case one of them exploded. Not unlike a patchwork of polders on a miniature scale, in fact.

"There were railway sidings on one side of the works, and goods trains used to come in with big loads of tree trunks chained to flatbed trucks, and long lines of wagons full of coal and sulphur. What came out of the factory on the other side left by road, in wooden boxes, packed into little vans." That's how you make explosives—you condense vast amounts of material into small packets and then liberate it on the battlefield.

I had this pair of ex-army binoculars on that trip, which I wish I still had. They had range-finding cross hairs in them. I used to gaze through the windshield of the car at the traffic in front and at the kilometers being gobbled up. I pretended we were in a tank and I was eliminating unnecessary traffic from the road.

That was when I was a boy; I will visit the polders again after the conference, but now here I am grown up, on my way to a rendezvous with my friends Hugo and Elena in Amsterdam. She has written to ask me if I am allergic to duck feather pillows, and if I will fax to her an outline of my dietary limits. As the ship approaches the low-lying land on which the oil tanks and wind turbines and container derricks of Europoort stand, I have a strong sense of the subtlety of sea-level management. Tiny changes in level—a few feet—make all the difference between safety and inundation. The well of the sea is contained by the dikes like a brimming wineglass, and the land, compared to the huge mass of the sea, looks, from the deck of the boat, to be nothing but a sliver.

The obvious way for a Londoner to go to Amsterdam is to climb on board an airbus and jet into Schipol—which is itself built on reclaimed land, on a polder called the Harlemermeer. There is something about jets descending below the horizon that appeals to a binoculars lover like me, most of all that moment when you see just the tail scooting along behind trees and houses, like a big building on the move. It is even more engaging when the jets are landing below sea level. The Harlemermeer is thirteen feet below sea level. The fact is that a great deal of the Netherlands is reclaimed, in work that has been going on since 1400. Draining the Harlemermeer—a meer is a shallow lake—was the dream of Amsterdammers for hundreds of years, but even they, the richest merchants in Europe, could not assemble the finances for the thousand-plus windmills that would have been required. It was only when steam power came along that they managed it. The Harlemermeer is the first great achievement of the modern generation of hydraulic engineers.

On the first evening, I am ensconced in Hugo and Elena's tiny center-city apartment up a flight of stairs so steep and long I daren't turn around when climbing them. I have been given the girls' room, which is okay by them, says Elena, as they've gone to a heavy metal concert in Dronten.

"What, out in Flevoland?" I ask. *Flevoland* is what they call the two newest Zuyder Zee polders, which are joined together down the middle. Dronten is one of the new towns there, and as clean and perfect as the new year.

"Of course," says Elena, "that's the only place where there's enough room." She is referring to the colossal population density of the Dutch mainland, where the whole countryside seems to be as closely packed as the center of Los Angeles. Driving from the Hague to Utrecht would be like driving from Burbank to Anaheim, were it not for the smiling cows and the cute church steeples everywhere you look. By contrast, Flevoland is as empty as Montana.

"I thought the polders were for agriculture. How can you go to all the trouble of reclaiming land only to use it for recreational purposes?"

"Recreation is a utility, most assuredly," explains Elena. "People would go mad without it." We are alone in the flat, and she pours me yet another glass of Graanjeneva, and there's a twinkle in her eyes.

"So what's new? How are Sally and Shahriar?"

"They treat each other like a pair of landscapes," I tell her. "Shah thinks he's found a goddess. He goes on and on about her perfection. Sally is more reticent. She thinks I'm upset."

"And are you?" she asks, coming to sit next to me on this big carpet bag they use for a floor cushion.

"Upset? When he treats her like a piece of sacred stone and she treats him like buried treasure? Not a bit! What happened to people and relationships?"

"You're not thinking of taking up poker, I hope," she says, shaking her glass so the ice rattles. "You can't hide anything."

"Sally thinks that sex is one of the wonders of the world," I say. "She should live in Amsterdam."

"Everyone thinks that. But it's the freedom that matters. The sex is just a part of the freedom."

When Hugo gets in, he is tired and excited from organizing the conference. The three of us sit on the floor like teenagers and eat Indonesian food from little heat-sealed polystyrene containers, and have an unwieldy conversation about landscape and machines, instigated by me. I need to get my lecture straightened out.

"Most machines have been invented to save time," I start out, "or at least to make more of it."

"Yes, I remember—*I reserve the right to distort time!*" says Hugo, quoting an English slogan from the permissive days. He is an Anglophile right down to his Burberry coat and his Itshide-soled brogues.

"And to distort distance," Elena says. "Don't forget the jumbo jets."

Hugo says they have someone from Switzerland who wants to do a sex machine talk at the conference. Elena winks at me. Hugo says they all stood around trying to decide what a Swiss sex machine would be like and concluded that it would probably wear a condom.

Elena starts to giggle through her mouthful of satay. "You know what the Dutch say about the Swiss," she explains. "They say, *If it's not forbidden, it's compulsory!*"

Hugo is grinning all over, too. "I wonder what a sex machine distorts," he says.

"What about children?" I suggest. "That's sex, having babies. Children are like little time sinks attached to your life." Is this me speaking, or is there someone else here stoned on Dutch gin? "You know, like those heat sinks on the back of your hi-fi."

"Oh, sure," says Elena. "You English. You have a machine for making babies, and you call it a sex machine."

After dinner we strolled out into the teeming streets of Amsterdam. Elena walked in the middle with her arms threaded through both of ours. It seemed old-fashioned at first, but then I got the sensation she was steering us like a pair of dummies. Hugo, certainly, was animated. He described a machine he'd read about in a Simon Schama book that used to be located in the street we were walking in, in a house of correction back in the seventeenth century. This prison was exclusively for vagrants, idlers, people who refused to work: a sort of Protestant experiment. Is it two hours of flogging a day or one hour in the stocks and one hour of flogging that eliminates idleness? Or three hours of Bible study? The machine in question is a small cell big enough for one human being and one hand-operated water pump.

"Water is cascaded in at the top, and it is only his continuous, strenuous activity at the pump that will stop the inmate from drowning! He is manacled to the floor by his ankles." It reminded me of Judge Jeffrys stapling felons to the river wall at Wapping and letting the incoming tide drown them. It is that subtlety of water level again. Your nostrils are the top of the dike; another centimeter, and you are done for.

"For heaven's sake!" said Elena, pulling on our elbows so our heads almost crashed together. "Stop talking about death!" She tugged my arm. "Have you seen the whores yet? Hugo, let's take him past the whores to the old church, and he can see a real-life Saanredam interior."

I had told them of my liking for Saanredam's paintings. They are super-real accounts of white Protestant church interiors, circa the golden age of Dutch painting. They seem like landscape paintings, full of minute detail receding into the distance. They are best looked at from six inches, just before your nose sets off the gallery burglar alarm, when their precision is as astonishing as a work of nature. So, I was on for visiting the old church. What I wasn't ready for was the streets full of whores we crossed to get to it, and Elena and Hugo laughed their heads off at my naive reaction to the open commerce of prostitution in that city. I am a novice, I admit it. I even believed the smiles the whores directed at me were real smiles. But then on St. Janstraat I caught the eye of a woman in a red corset leaning against a door. Her face was covered in pink blusher. Her fingers were covered in little leather rings. Her eyes were as blank and inward as a beast of burden's— she looked at me with the same dumb stare as a cow. I see what they mean by the oldest profession—her eyes looked like those of a species far older than my own.

The next day was the first day of the conference, and Hugo was bustling with nerves. A small audience had assembled for the first event, which turned out to be a slide lecture of work—paintings of cows in the landscape—by a man Hugo introduced as Rodney. More cows! Rodney stood in front of his paintings, daring us to ask questions. He was tall, good looking, and as erudite as a witch doctor, so people were frightened of him. His cow paintings were really pictures of Texas. He had painted a cattle-breeding landscape of flat red fields and distant barbed-wire fences. The reason this was a *Machines in the Landscape* event is that the works were not paintings, in fact, but narrowly three-dimensional constructions in which the canvas had been worked so hard that it was indistinguishable from cowhide. The works had a great deal of mechanical ingenuity woven into them, little wheels and rails like experimental bombsights, which made them rock, very gently, from side to side. There was something deep and seismographic about the movements, although the images themselves are as strong as oxen.

"Ask me questions if you like," said Rodney to the silent, petrified audience. "I don't know what to say about this stuff." Neither did the rest of the room: it was just too damn good to penetrate.

"I was looking at a cow yesterday," I said, into the silence. I meant the St. Janstraat whore. Everyone held their breath, and all I could hear while I framed the second half of the sentence was the whirring of the projector fan, keeping the bulb cool. "I looked into her eyes, and they seemed to stare out of the deep past at me. She seemed fossilized, she looked so primitive. She seemed as steady as the past itself, this cow— so what is this rocking movement you are trying to catch?"

Rodney swept the question aside with a disgusted shake of his head, and said it was kind of a pun—"Have you never heard of a rocking *horse*?" This is why he is so frightening. He says, go on—ask a question—and then when you do, he heaves a sigh and raises his eyes to the ceiling as if to say, You dolt! Do you understand *nothing*?

He pressed the blip on the remote control, and the next pair of images on the screen was a pair of landscapes—both huge flat dusty plains. Texas, the country around San Angelo, on the left; the plateau above Johannesberg on the right, where the Boers herded their cattle and pitched their stockades. He had an interesting commentary on the Boers and the cowboys both herding cows across raw land in the 1860s, branding cattle as though they were staking land claims, as though the huge herds were a sort of land on the hoof. And he said he had nothing to say! But then he went on, "Out in these places there is no middle ground—everything is either the distant horizon or it's detail, right up close." He said he was stressing the "disurbanity of the plains." His next slides showed what cities are made of. Two Victorian English paintings: on the left, O'Connor's *Pentonville, Looking West, Evening,* where the outline of St. Pancras sits in the mist behind the detailed rendering of Pentonville Road looking like a painted backdrop— "all middle ground," says Rodney, "even the horizon." On the right was William Powell Frith's *Derby Day,* with its tumultuous mass of the bourgeoisie at play. I got the point. The far horizon and the things in reach are a consequence of the empty plain. The middle ground is where the mass of people stand, with their conceit and their confusion and their endless fascination with each other. You get it in crowded places, like the Epsom Downs on Derby Day. You get it in cities. Rodney prefers the unambiguous life of the prairie dog.

———————

That afternoon I am standing in a perfect one-room museum of Dutch landscape painting. It is a genre like English sixteenth-century harpsichord music. It is complex, profound, and forever interesting albeit bound within its single dimension with hoops of steel. This little museum has four walls, one with a door in it, the other three with one painting each hanging in the center. Everything is smooth and white, except for the floor, which is a clatter of red and yellow quarry tiles laid at random, like the Saanredam church. The light comes from an elaborate wooden cupola high up in the roof. The first painting is of the inundation of the Waal and Maas estuaries in the great flood of November 1421—the St. Elizabeth's Day flood—and painted by an anonymous person known as the *Master of the St. Elizabeth's Day Flood Panel.* The survivors of the flood, in which thousands of people died, are tumbling into passing boats like bodies into the plague carts, dragging their sodden belongings behind them. Some of them stayed in the boats and became meer-pirates, sort of waterborne highwaymen. The land was not reclaimed for centuries—the painting was done about seventy years after the flood itself, when the meer had established reed marshes around its edge and was the home of seabirds and waders. The whole landscape, from nearby to right out on the horizon, is full of the spires of the churches of villages doomed by the flood, sticking out of the water like wrecks. It reminds me of this *empty middle ground* theory for flat, rural landscapes—because it shows the opposite.

The second Dutch landscape is one of those Piet Mondrian grids. This is the man who set about painting the flat Dutch landscape—reduced for the sake of the new century to one dike, one tree—but who slowly swung the picture plane through ninety degrees in the course of his abstraction experiments until we are looking straight down, as if from the air. It is a landscape of the grid of drainage dikes. This is not my observation: it is the sort of art criticism that takes a perception of the first order to see, but once it has been seen, the rest of us can join in. For example: the white backgrounds that Mondrian uses, that's not neutral, that white. It's super dense, in the way that white is a compaction of all the colors in the spectrum from red through violet, in the way that the Dutch landscape itself is dense, full of people and technique. Full of tactics, a manufactured landscape. The urban countryside: *all middle ground.*

I never stay in front of Mondrians for long. I think abstraction is such a desperate game. To go back to Rodney for a moment, to when some other brave soul tried to tackle him on the subject of figurative art—no doubt thinking of the similarity between painting cows in Texas and painting sheep in Dorset, as one of those Victorian narrative painters Rodney despised had done, in fact.

"Look, I work on my own, in a studio miles away from anywhere that has any . . . *art* in it. I need the company of the figurative. Abstraction is something for *schools,* for café society artists who get all the company they need from talking out the work of the day over glasses of absinthe. If you work on your own, take it from me, be figurative." This is from an artist whose constructions are as realistic and as profound as the ancient Greek Animaxander's model of the universe with its cylindrical earth. It's as though he is working toward the figurative from a culture that has become heavily abstracted, and having to work as hard to find it as Mondrian did going in the reverse direction!

It is as quiet as a prairie in the little museum. On the third wall is my favorite of all the Dutch landscapes ever, annotated by experts as the first realistic one, a drawing by Hendrik Golzius of the view out across the dunes to the west of Haarlem, a pen-and-ink drawing he made in 1603. He was one of the first to go out into the terrain itself to draw. It is a task, to draw flat landscapes, especially these Dutch ones with so much middle ground in them. The job is to make a series of minutely differentiated horizontal lines across the paper, starting with the most critical of all, the most dense, which is the horizon. It may even have a slight curve, like the entasis on a Periclean temple. It will have buildings on it, this horizon, perhaps even a whole city. The eagerness of our human eyes exaggerates little facets of interest at long range, so the drawing will have to simulate that, too. The middle ground may also have trees, and dikes that are but two or three meters above the flat, and the ferociously foreshortened curves of roads, and the bottom quarter of the picture will start to show shrubs and grasses distinct from the trees, and people, and the detail of the roofs of buildings: but we are still on a basic matrix of horizontal lines, perhaps as little as half a millimeter apart.

I think the Golzius drawing is so perfect because it was built up one line at a time, lines so close together his tongue must have been clamped between his teeth to steady every single stroke. Just as the dikes were built: one spadeful of mud at a time, patted down and heeled into place by clog, over and over again as patiently as the sea's waves are relentless. The Dutch landscape is a phenomenon of human effort, as though all the fields were buildings as well as the buildings—as though the entire country were an urban conglomeration. No wonder, Rodney, the flatlands here have so much middle ground!

There are four polders in the IJsselmeer, the new freshwater lake that has been made from the Zuyder Zee. They are called the Wieringer, the Nord-Oost, the Zuid-Oost, and the Zuid. The whole plan, however, is for five: the last, the Markerwaard, has been held up since 1970 by indecision and, it seems, fatigue. The project to dam the Zuyder Zee and reclaim the shallower two-thirds of it is a twentieth-century plan. It was put together at the beginning of the century by Cornelius Lely, the inheritor of the long Dutch experience of hydraulic engineering, and the plan was finally acted on by the Dutch Parliament in 1918, after big floods two years earlier. The Wieringer polder was dry by 1930; the big barrier dam across the mouth of the Zuyder Zee, the Afsluitdijk, or Out-Sluice Dike, was finished in 1932. The Nord-Oost polder was dry in 1942, the Zuid-Oost in 1957, the Zuid in 1968. It takes about a year to pump the water out of a twenty-kilometer-square polder lying around four meters deep, and about twenty years of progressive deep draining and special cropping after that before the land is in a condition to support farms. So it is only now, at the tail end of the century, that the last polder is coming into use. The railway across Flevoland was completed in 1988.

The project was conceived at a time when social engineering was the way great minds thought, and the polders were built all through the National Socialist and New Deal years between the wars, and in the progressive spirit of the new Europe that prevailed through to 1980. Film of the early work camps, with men in striped cotton suits sponging soup out of tin bowls with hunks of bread, and grappling with huge stones against a background of steel derricks and clouds of steam, is film of another world. It is incomprehensible that a native Dutch work force of that kind could be created now. They did it then against a background of depression, labor camps, refugees, and big totalitarian movements; they were rewarded for their toil with plots of farming land. They were called pioneers, the first settlers. They lived in an all new society that makes the suburban settlements of our big cities look as dense and historical as the city centers themselves. If the last polder is ever completed, it will be done by private enterprise, by contractors working to tight profit plans, with a safety-helmeted work force protected by legislation, who are interested in the money, not the land. It will probably be 90 percent recreational, or covered in forest for paper pulp. Elena will not be able to say "But recreation is a utility, too," because contracts will hold sway over the land.

You can stand at Lelystad Haven in the August sunshine with the five-thousand-hectare reed beds of the nature reserve behind you, and look out across the IJsselmeer at the perimeter dike of this missing polder. That at least had to be built as part of the complex water management of the area. It strikes out across the lake toward Enkhuizen, which stands on land poldered in the seventeenth century, twenty miles away. From this vantage point the road on the top of the dike disappears into the haze at about five miles; you can just see distant trucks inching their way along it, apparently driving on water, the steep sides of the containers they are hauling looking like rectangular boat sails. There are plenty of these big horizons to be had. On the other side of the nature reserve

A secondary canal on Zuid-Oost Flevoland, the Netherlands. Photograph by the author.

you can see across a patchwork of arable farms, whose vast fields are all being busily harvested. The horizon now is eight miles, made of the trees that line the central distributor road that runs the length of the polder. There are trees everywhere on the polders, in plantations, along the roads, and sheltering the farmsteads in thick clumps dotted across the open landscape, maybe a thousand yards apart. Most of the trees are poplars, which grow fast and wick up lots of water. They bear their leaves on thin stems, and the leaves are silver gray on the undersides. Every time there is a gust of wind a silver shimmer spreads over the whole landscape as the slight stems give way.

My plan was to cross the Markerwaarddijk to Enkhuizen, and then travel up the edge of the IJsselmeer to the barrier dam, which separates the lake from the North Sea. As I pedaled, lights burning, along into the sea mist that hung over the Maarkerwaarddijk road, a flock of cormorants rose from the water on one side and crossed to the other. The flock was maybe three hundred strong. When the leaders took off, they seemed to pull the others along in lines, like wool unraveling from a skein, and they flapped their way slowly across the dike and settled on the other side. The leaders arrived before the last had left, so they formed a little bridge of black specks across the road. The cormorants are one of the avian success stories of the new regime, because they love the long stretches of close-to-the-water vantage points the dikes afford. The young herring gulls don't seem to be so lucky. They don't expect to find trucks moving at 120 kilometers per hour in open water, and the sides of the road are littered with carcasses.

From Enkhuizen at the end of the dike, I moved on north through land poldered three hundred years ago, in the golden age. The dikes there have steep sides, with no road along the top, so there is no view of the expanse of the IJsselmeer as you pass the little ribbon of buildings along the edge of the dike: little houses with privet hedges, little shops selling ice cream, little churches held together by iron wall ties wrought in numbers that spell out the date of construction—1 6 6 7. And round wooden windmills, obsolete now, stand as still as crucifixes by the road.

The point of coming up this way was to see the experimental polder—the Proefpolder—built at the outset of the Zuyder Zee scheme to test dike construction methods. It was built at Andijk, where the old steep dike is made of consolidated clay, heeled into place and fortified with wooden piles. The new type—if 1918 is new—is a machine-made, clay-cored sand-bank faced with stone. It has a much wider base, and hence a shallower face, than the old dike, to take the power out of the big sea swash. *Swash* is the distance a breaking wave travels up the beach, the distance over which it spreads its destructive power. It is not the direct battering that breaks the dyke, but overtopping, when the flow of water sweeps away the inland face, so swash length is a vital thing to accommodate, and to do that you must make an estimate of the highest possible tides. There is a four-hundred-year-old groove carved into the side of the town hall at Amsterdam that represents the sea-level datum for all these calculations. The maximum level predicted by the Zuyder Zee study is just about twelve feet above this line, so the enclosing barrier dike rises to twenty-five to take care of the swash. The Proefpolder at Andijk was the test bed for these new big dykes. One advantage of them is that they can carry roads, and the feeling of elation when the old road suddenly climbs up onto the new dike and gives a view of the IJsselmeer makes old Andijk, stuck behind its dike like a soldier in a trench, seem blinkered and provincial. It's a nice little paradox, because the Amsterdammers, who live in a city that is free by ancient charter, feel just the same about the polder pioneers who went to live on Flevoland.

"How can they live where they do?" said Elena, giving me the address of family friends with whom her daughters were staying, and whom I was supposed to visit on my way back across the other side of the IJsselmeer. "Life out there is all turnips and sky. When I talk to them now, it's as if their brains have turned to clay."

The Proefpolder is not big—maybe one kilometer across. Now there is a holiday camp on it, which is plagued by swarms of midges that breed in the still water of the drainage ditches. They dance in the air in swarms thicker than a hailstorm, at head height, too, so they get in your eyes and your mouth and your hair when you try to get past them. I never came across them anywhere else on the polders.

The Wieringer polder to the north, almost at the point where the barrier dike strikes out for the opposite side of the IJsselmeer, is the oldest of the four polders. The trees have grown so big in fifty years that you keep having to remind yourself it's new land. The farmsteads that spread out across the flatland—all with the same red pitched roofs, all surrounded by a thick dark windbreak of trees—are like ships in berths. Flocks of starlings almost as big as the sky wheel and settle in these trees in noisy throngs. Later, on the Afsluitdijk itself, I found a solitary starling working the tourists for food. It was standing begging on the Afsluitdijk monument. It was a tragedy—the lonely bird reminded me of an exiled Sophoclean Greek—a gregarious being cut off from the sustenance of his fellows' company. At flocking time a starling has but one song, I would have explained had I had a child with me. It is a chorus called *Us*.

The little tragedy was soon forgotten in the face of the heroism evinced by the big dike. The memorial built over the last section to be closed in 1932 has a tower that you can climb and from which you can look out across the IJsselmeer, on one side, and the open sea, on the other. This is where I met the windblown cyclists heading in the other direction. In the distance from the top of the tower you can just make out the sluice gates that open at low tide to let the penned-in water from the IJsselmeer drain out. Fresh water, remember, fed into the IJsselmeer by the rivers to the south; the fishers inside the dike who used to fish for place and herring now fish for eel and perch. The dike was made to prevent floods, but this freshwater reservoir is almost reason enough in itself to have built the dike. In drought years, when the rest of Europe is gasping for water, the level in the IJsselmeer is allowed to rise by a mere foot—and then is trickled back into the drainage channels to irrigate the reclaimed land. In dry weather on the polders you are constantly coming across sparkling channels of water, part of the whole daily drama of water management, the sound of the water moving inland filling the air with luxury. I am lyrical about it because there is such beauty in utility: the big dike is the evidence of such clear strategic thinking that its very side effects are a boon that others would kill for.

After crossing the Afsluitdijk, I made camp for the night at a village called Zurich. Behind me was the North Sea; before me lay the old flatlands of Friesland. Hugo had advised me not to stop there, not even to buy a packet of chewing gum. He said they speak Friesian and only Friesian, and they despise the English as much as they despise the Germans.

"Friesland was the last place to be liberated in 1945. The Allies were more interested in racing the Russians to Berlin than in making a detour to the north," he said. "The town of Delfzijl, on the Dutch side of the Eems estuary, was still in German hands when Berlin fell."

The little children of Zurich, uncontaminated by this memory, were friendly enough. They gathered around to look at my bike and offered me candy and thought I was an idiot because I couldn't understand what they were saying. When their father came out to see what the commotion was, it turned out that he was driving across Friesland the next day with a cargo of sheep, and he could take me all the way to Lemmer, at the tip of the second polder, the Nord-Oost. Friesland is old polder land—in fact it has the oldest dikes in it, heeled into place in the twelfth century—but I was in search of the new. I took the lift gladly and sat next to the sheep farmer without saying a word for twenty-five miles. All the way we moaned to each other about the heavy traffic, using sign language.

It was a relief to be back on the dead straight tracks and big open fields of the new polder, where the edge is defined by the ruler-flat edge of the perimeter dike. Back to the regular sequence of ditches, the primaries at four-kilometer intervals, the secondaries feeding into them every five hundred meters, and, underground, land drains every ten to fifteen, depending on the clay-to-sand ratio of the soil. The main ditches drain into a canal, which runs around the polder and is emptied by pumping stations either into the IJsselmeer or into the smaller lakes that act as a buffer between old land and new, to stop the old land from drying out. Everywhere the steady pattern of farmsteads, lines of windbreak trees, and big flat fields is repeated. Everyone drives with their lights on because, without bends, distances are so difficult to judge, and the back roads are just sixteen feet wide. When a vehicle meets another one coming the other way, both cars get their nearside wheels onto the shoulder and rattle past, headlights blazing.

The whole place seems so managed and serviceable that it takes a while for the freedom of it to soak in. The emptiness, the big chunks of parkland, the cycle tracks threaded through the towns and villages, the proximity of water. Above all it is the newness, not just as in *recently built,* but as in *never there before.* The persistent realization that the sea is being held back so you can walk on the sea bed, that the water if it broke in would be two fathoms deep and way over your head, has a breathtaking quality to it. I don't need to evoke the miracle of the Red Sea parting, because it is more real than that. It is the miracle of something made out of nothing. The miracle of growth.

FLEVOLAND

A long time ago, when the Zuyder Zee was the Celtic heartland, people lived in little clusters on the marshes, on mounds of mud called *Terpen* that they had raised above sea level. The marshes were a good place to live—abundant reeds for weaving houses, fish and fowl in plenty, swimming past the terp There is an engaging theory that this paradise was the playground of the Acheans, the same Acheans who besieged Troy. The theory goes that Troy was in fact a Celtic city not far from Cambridge in the marshes of eastern England, and that the ancient Greeks were not from Asia Minor, but were the members of a Celtic exodus from what is now the Netherlands, following a catastrophic flood around 900 B.C. They took their ballads with them to Greece and renamed their new land after the old. In this theory, the Aegean Sea is a kind of Homeric theme park, and the author—a Dutchman— says that Homer himself came from Middleburg, in the Netherlands. He cites the Homeric references to seals and mist as being North Sea phenomena, not Mediterranean ones; he says all those horses suggest a Celtic culture, not a Mediterranean island one, and shows, by a detailed analysis of sailing times given in the *Iliad* and the *Odyssey,* that none of it makes sense in the Aegean topography that bears the names, but all of it fits the islands of the North Sea and the Atlantic. Is it all crazy? Ideas like this at least make us review the beds of our own knowledge, like looking at the world through a different filter. My grandmother once showed me how different the world looked through a green wine bottle. She called it *looking at the world through rose-leaf-colored glasses.*

The polder people take their Celtic heritage seriously, as only pioneers can. Like those Californians who show you the Wells Fargo trail at the bottom of the canyon, saying, "Whoops! Look out for rattlesnakes down here!" On Flevoland new housing schemes built on the edge of the little spick-and-span towns are sentimentally christened *Terpen* by their marketing agents, as though the old pattern of settlement still somehow survives. The few islands that were scattered across the Zuyder Zee and were engulfed by the new land are carefully preserved in outline. Their old sea walls and their gentle rising forms stick out of the surrounding flatness like bones on a tarsus. When I knock on the door of Elena's friends' house in Biddinghuizen, Oost Flevoland, a village six miles south of Dronten, I am expecting the clodhopping bores she has described. I know that living in a small town is a battle to achieve the middle ground of convention. Whether you are trying to preserve your identity or bury it, life is one strenuous striking of attitude after another, and the strain shows in the faces of small-town people. So, with

**The line of the horizon is visible beneath the trees lining the
Vogelweg on Zuid Flevoland, the Netherlands. Photograph by
the author.**

two bouts of prejudice riding my shoulders, mine and
Elena's, I was not prepared for the soft beauty of the red-
haired woman who opened the door, or the glimpse of sunlit
plants in the garden behind the house, or the two big
Labrador dogs, or her husband descending the stairs to fill the
little hall with his beard, or the children appearing covered in
mud with no clothes on, or the challenging similarity of Elena
and Hugo's twin daughters, sitting in the room I was ushered
into, wreathed in clouds of smoke, examining a range of red
hair dyes laid out across the table. I had the impression of
having landed somewhere capacious after a great slide.

   I was drawn straight into the merits of the different hair
dyes. It is this Celtic push again—"Batavian women had red
hair," says one of the twins.

"Not like Beatrix's," says the other, and Beatrix smiles because her red hair is real, "but dyed with herbs."

We try, with our combined half knowledge, to unravel the mystery behind Celtic women's using henna on their hair. Where did they get it from? Beatrix says *Phoenecian traders,* I say *They grew it—their climate was warmer,* but Beatrix's husband Frederick informs us that it was not Henna—Al'canna—but another plant altogether, Alcanetta, or *Anchusa tinctoria,* which also yields a red dye, and which was grown by the Celts. I pick up a packet of dye with a photo of a perfect woman swinging her thick auburn mane at the camera. The contents appear to be chemical compounds, not herbs, so they have Greek-based names, like geological terms.

"Why is it that geologists use Greek and biologists Latin?" I ask, but my question goes unanswered. The conversation is terminated by a sudden burst of hard-core metal music that cascades from the loudspeakers like Armageddon and makes the dogs put their ears back in alarm. Beatrix and Frederick are for turning it down, the twins for turning it up. One of them leaps out of her chair and squats by the speaker and shouts, "Here! Now! You see!" and the bass drum patterns multiply so fast they sound like an air raid.

"It's a machine, a drum machine, isn't it?" I yell, above the din.

"Not at all!" says the other twin. She pulls out a crumpled magazine photo of the drummer—a burly Texan called Vinnie with a fierce glint in his eyes and sweat pouring down his face. She kisses it and twirls around as though this is 1958 and she is kissing a picture of Bobby Vee.

"Nothing changes," says Beatrix, smiling. But those triplet kick-drum riffs are unbelievable. No one was doing *that* in

1958. Vinnie must have the toughest, most flexible ankles in the world. He must be built like a machine.

I came to the Netherlands to talk about machines in the landscape; in one sense the polders and their sluice dams are landscape-sized machines, and this subject of machines doing what humans do, and vice versa, is definitely part of all that. I remember when the Grand Master was beaten at chess by a computer and declared, his big gray Russian face creased in gloom, that the end of human civilization had dawned. I recall a story about the arrival of the first steam-powered trench digger among the squads building the Great Western Railway in England in 1865. The strongest man challenged it to a dual, and it was decided that two parallel trenches would be dug, one by the man and one by the digger. Although the man started well and was ahead at noon, by mid-afternoon the relentless energy of the machine began to count against human bravado and he was forced to throw in the towel. These are sad stories of men and machines, but they are inevitable somehow, like the ending of the suicide pacts between master and slaves, or like the emptying out of small-town centers into shopping malls. On the other hand, we have this music—it could be made by machines, but the point is, it's not—or the space shuttle program—it could all be done by machines, but what for? There is a beauty in human ambition. These polders, now, they are like this music: monotonous but profound.

So we drank and laughed and talked like city folk, and I couldn't see that turnip-head theory of Elena's one bit. At the end of the evening, I settled down to sleep on a couch still warm with the warmth of bodies.

"If the dogs bother you, just say *Ga Demand*," said Beatrix.

"Ga-de-mand," I repeated.

"It means go to bed. They'll do what you tell them." It is amazing enough to me that dogs obey human commands. To give them phonetic commands and see them respond is uncanny, like learning to drive a computer. In the morning when I woke they were both still lying as if asleep, looking at me out of one eye, waiting for me to release them from their beds—but I didn't have the right words.

<hr>

The twins had come to Flevoland in Elena's Beetle, and after a breakfast of cheese and salami they drove me and my bike and Frederick into Lelystad, so we could catch the yellow double-decker commuter train out to Rotterdam. There was a stream of cars all the way there like a rush hour anywhere else in the Western world. The brand-new systems of Flevoland are up to it, though, so the rush is not made of jams but of long necklaces of headlights as far as you can see. There was a wind up that morning, and as we passed the Flevocentrum windfarm the big white turbines were flailing around at a terrific speed.

"They look like arms waving in the snakepit," said the twin in the passenger seat, and she made the metal sign of peace and waved her arms from side to side. So did the one driving.

"Hey, cut that out," said Frederick. He pointed out the digital display board standing by the road, which says something like *this is the community electricity* and shows the megawatts being generated and the wind force at that moment. I was due back at Hoek van Holland in the afternoon to board the ferry back to England, and I wondered aloud what force 6 was like, in the open North Sea. Isn't force 6 more than halfway to hurricane force 12?

"Flevoland is a windy place," said Frederick. "It's because we are flat and low lying and by open water. You've seen the windbreak trees around the farmsteads? But you see also that we harness the wind to help pump water—the Dutch always have, although now it's electrical, not mechanical." His voice was thin and serious in the sleepy morning unreality of the car ride. He nodded with pleasure at the strings of combine harvesters spread across the land, saying that the harvest was early enough to guarantee success of the winter crop.

"When we first drain this land, it is just gray salty mud. We sow reed seed from the air and let it grow for a few years, then after harvesting the reed, we plough the roots back in and start with the next stage: hardy crops like rape and fescue, and then after another few years it is good enough to use for corn and grass for milk cows."

"With all those reeds, why don't you thatch the roofs?" I asked him.

"Because there was no one here when the reeds were here! This isn't land with its own long-term character; this is all new, remember. It's like California, everything's new. No— better than California, because the earth is new, too!"

The twins snort with derision from the front of the car. "Frederick, you speak out of your bum," says one. "What do you old men know about what's new?" says the other. "The polder works are an ecological crime. We have altered the natural equilibrium of three and a half thousand square kilometers of estuarine landscape, home to fishes, birds, and plants that can no longer live there."

"What for?" says her sister. "So a few farmers with heads as thick as their clogs can grow a few more turnips?"

"And how do they do that? By spraying the whole landscape with insecticides. It's an agricultural desert!"

"Of course, you have polder land in England too," says Frederick, trying to change the subject. "The fens. Did you know they were drained by the Dutch?"

Yes I did, I told him, and I also know the stories of dissent and revolt that is the seventeenth-century dispossession of the marsh people by land improvers.

"That's right!" says a chorus from the front seat. "They used to live in a land of plenty, full of game and fresh fish, and now they have to live in houses made out of concrete planks and eat out of refrigerators."

"Why don't you drain the Wash?" Frederick asks me. "That would be all new land—no history to worry about."

I can't answer him. Why don't the Italians polder the Po estuary and save Venice? Why don't the Bangladeshi polder the mouths of the Ganga and save lives? Why, for that matter, don't the Dutch drain the Markerwaard and finish the job? Could it be the opposition of the next generation, as voiced by the red-headed pair in black T-shirts in the front of this little yellow car?

"As a matter of fact," says Frederick, "a large part of the South Polder has been set aside for a nature reserve." He leans forward. "You'll drive past it on your way back to Amsterdam," he tells the twins. He says that in the center of the reserve is an absolute sanctuary, where no human ever goes, not even wardens. They call it the *Silent Core.* "I suppose you two want to live in a land that is always being flooded by the sea. That's what the IJsselmeer scheme is about, flood control. The new land is just a bonus."

"As a matter of fact," say the twins in unison, "we want to live in Texas!"

As we swing onto the ramp for Lelystad, making for the station, the car goes quiet. I fall to thinking about another big hydraulic landscape, the Elan Valley reservoirs in central Wales. Water for the West Midlands conurbation is collected here in a series of mountain lakes created at the beginning of the twentieth century by a series of dams across the rivers Claerwen and Elan. The Cambrian mountains are not themselves anything like the Dutch lowlands, but the Elan Valley reservoirs are a big utilitarian landscape, like the polders; based on hydraulic engineering, like the polders; and, like them, have the strategic grace to confer a recreational boon on the landscape that benefits everyone who goes there. It is the beauty of the five dams themselves that gives the landscape such power. They are not great because they are huge, like the Upper Volta dam, whose vast mass of contained water produced earth tremors in the countryside around it as the water levels rose. They are not *tours de force* like the pencil-thin concrete bows jammed into crevices in the Italian Alps. The best of them, the Pennygarreg, is a high granite wall across which water cascades like an enormous fountain. The wall has projecting blocks of stone set in it to break up the cascade and fill the valley with mist and rainbow colors. When you stand below it, you feel the quantity of water coming down as an animal experience of plenty. The noise of it takes you back to your beginnings. It warms you with your own internal heat.

Now, here is little Lelystad, the capital of Flevoland, named after the engineer who dreamed it up, Cornelius Lely. So new it's half built still, with its cracking little steel-and-glass station and its shiny rails and trains that leave and arrive on the dot. People glide around on upright bicycles with saddles that look like cushions, towing stroller trailers filled with chubby children. The roads are paved with red brick. A gang of Asian boys kick their heels in the market square, going nowhere. The last thing I see on the polders, just before the bridge that takes the train over the strand of water that separates Flevoland from the rest of Holland, is a farm girl breaking a horse on the end of a long training rope. The field behind her is full of beautiful chestnut mares. Why do they have horses here, in this land of big tractors? Is it for recreational riding? Or are the horses still more evidence of utility—a reserve against the day when we all run out of gas?

III
TOPOGRAPHY

An angel on the memorial to Major General Robert Ross, St. Paul's Cathedral, London. Photograph by John Shepheard.

6
VISION

THE LONDON BASIN

How far can you see? What has to be demolished for you to see what you want to see? Does what you want to see exist yet? If not, can you see it in your imagination?

VISION

THE LONDON BASIN

────────────── THE RIVER ──────────────

It is a warm June evening. I have just visited the Palace of Westminster as a tour leader with seventy Koreans, to show them the hall King Richard built in 1399. My lecture about the roof takes forty-five minutes and is highly technical, which the Koreans like. They are the friendliest bunch I've ever toured with. They call me *sir.* They regard the coming-into-being of their economic miracle, and its catchy slogan, *Twenty-Twenty!*—it means both perfect vision and the target year for universal prosperity in Korea—as passionately as the ancient Greeks waking up in the dawn of Homer's light regarded theirs: as if this empire-building thing had never been seen in the world before. Now, here they are, standing with a son of what used to be Great Britain, on Westminster Bridge. Gazing across at what the Great British used to call the *Heart of Empire:* the city of London.

There must be people reflecting on lost empire all over the world. Old Austrians in Vienna wondering why their government has to buy secondhand fighters from the Canadian air force. Old Turks in Istanbul remembering the days when their city was the crossroads of world trade. Old Britons remembering when their empire stretched farther than Ceasar's—but this is no time to get misty eyed. I am

Canaletto, *View from Somerset Gardens,* **looking toward London Bridge. Courtesy Courtauld Institute Galleries, London.**

guiding a party of tourists, and I need to concentrate. I need my tips. I steer them down the steps under the glorious statue of Boudicca in her chariot, bronze harnesses straining under the urgency of her steeds, made ninety years ago by the sculptor Thomas Thorneycroft, using a modeling skill now lost, alas, as surely as a penny down a drain—but this is no time to get misty eyed. We are making for Westminster Pier, where we will get on a boat and float down the river to Greenwich, where the Koreans will be stunned by the Painted Hall and will excitedly stand astride the meridian line of nought degrees, one foot in the Western hemisphere, one foot in the Eastern.

While we are waiting for the boat, I show them the view of St. Paul's Cathedral, a view that is protected by law. No one is allowed to build in such a way as to obscure the view of the dome from this spot. They are intrigued and assume that it is the sacredness of the place that is being preserved, but it is not exactly that. There are nine protected sightlines of St. Paul's—and three of the Palace of Westminster—all from the hills around the London Basin, except for this one, in the shadow of Big Ben. It looks northeast across the bend of the river called King's Reach and glimpses St. Paul's standing on its own little hill in the middle of the city, through the gap between the Festival Hall and the Shell Building. There is such a wealth of history in all these names! I am just starting on an explanation of *Festival* when a beggar emerges from the tunnel running through the embankment and pushes his red face into mine and asks me for money. I am all misty eyed, and he asks me for money. It's no good. Three hundred years of folk memory descend upon me. *Hark, Hark!* it goes, *the dogs do bark, the beggars are coming to town!* I felt ashamed for him, because I guess that in Korea a man would sooner sell bottle caps picked up from the gutter than beg outright. Up close, my man's face is not just red. It has the bloody purple sheen of nights spent sleeping rough, and he reeks of urine, like an animal. The Koreans fall silent and watch me turn him away with grim embarrassment on their faces. I turn to them and shrug my shoulders: within sight of the richest financial center the world has ever seen—a sight protected by law, mind you—and with the mother of Parliaments standing behind us, here is this beggar, rubbing in the eternal disparity between an empire and its people.

I should not have shrugged. I should have taken him by his purple hands, all soft with disuse, and introduced him personally to my party from the Pacific Rim. They are looking daggers at me. One of them takes out his wallet and hands the beggar a ten-pound note. The poor man takes it and holds it in both hands, staring at it—he is not checking it for counterfeit, like the news vendors do, he is amazed—and then, one by one, all the others, all seventy of them, do exactly the same thing. Not a word from me, just seventy ten-pound notes passing from their wallets into his filthy hands. He looks at me and smiles, cluthing his enormous wad of money.

"That's my tips you've got there," I tell him, exaggerating, and he smiles again—a wide open smile, as wide as a Cadillac—and he shrugs his shoulders.

The river Thames meanders through London for twenty miles. In the painter Canaletto's time, 1750, the river at Waterloo Bridge was half as wide again as it is now. A century later, a new sewer was constructed along the North Bank of the Thames, to pick up the sewage-laden outfalls of the river Tyburn at Westminster and the river Fleet at Blackfriars and to carry them out to the new treatment plants to the east of London. This was the Victoria Embankment, and the engineering works included a new underground railway alongside the sewer and a new road on top: the whole thing reduces the width of the river to around three hundred yards.

It is noon, and the incident of the beggar is behind us, and the seventy Koreans and I are packing one of the tourist boats that works the river between Westminster and Greenwich. As we putter downstream past the embankment, the tourist guides pick out the interesting monuments along the way: the monuments to the Royal Air Force, to the engineer who built the sewer, to the submariners of two world wars, to George the Fifth, after whom the King's Reach is named. We pass Cannon Street station, which used to have an enormous glass roof, a Victorian wonder of the world. The roof was dismantled in World War II and stored in a warehouse in the Kent countryside to protect it from the blitz. Unfortunately, although the station itself survived unscathed, the warehouse, and everything in it, was destroyed by a direct hit from a wayward flying bomb. All this is relayed in an exaggerated Shoreditch cockney voice by the tour guide, who holds his microphone to his lips and whispers into it like Rod Stewart, to the utter confusion of the Koreans. He calls the flying bomb a *doodlebug*. They learned to speak English from American tapes and don't understand a word this Londoner is saying. Too bad. I don't translate: I tell them instead what really matters about this riverboat trip. The city of London is a congested place. It lacks the broad avenues and axial systems of Paris or Washington, so it is hard to get a view of the whole thing. You have three choices: you climb the few towers the security guards haven't yet closed down; you go up on the hills around, five miles away; or you come down here to the Thames, where the open expanse of the river gives you wide, panoramic views.

These are the views that Canaletto painted: looking downstream from the terrace of Old Somerset House—with the dome of St. Paul's, then about thirty years completed, dominating the skyline—and looking upstream from the same place toward the brand-new Westminster Bridge, where Westminster Abbey is the dominant sight. Although the pictures are far more complex than this in what they show—for example, the white bulk of the Inigo Jones Banqueting House, built in 1622, which sticks up above Whitehall looking so modern (which is to say *antiquarian radical*) in comparison to Westminster Hall, built in 1399, which is also visible in the painting and which, with its modular symmetries, was as modern in its day as anything could be, because Chaucer advised the architect and Chaucer had the Renaissance first-hand from Petrarch—where was I? The Koreans don't know, although they are still listening politely. Oh yes—there are two Londons, the city of London and the city of Westminster, and Canaletto painted them both. I think it is useful to hold these simple armatures of thought in one's mind, although the world has become so much obscured since 1750.

The expanse of the river introduced London to its first panoramas, produced by topography-mad Dutchmen in the seventeenth century, who painted what they saw from the top of Southwark Cathedral. A century later, Canaletto's vantage point from the terrace of Old Somerset House was about twelve feet above water level and has been replaced now by the embankment, which gives, were it not for the trees, almost the same view. From a boat on the river itself, the views are slightly but thrillingly different. There is a strange luxury in looking up at the land from a river. We could be travelers on the Amazon, or the crew of that patrol boat in *Apocalypse Now* making their way up the Mekong into Cambodia.

I can remember being on the clay beach of one of the Suffolk estuaries in the middle of a windless night with a bright full moon, when the tide had ebbed to its lowest point. The river there is wider than the Thames. It was absolutely calm, so flat calm I could hear the rustle of the crabs under water. I knelt down to get my face as close as I could to the surface, and looked up, stretching my eyebrows, across the river to the far side. I felt as though I had come to the fundament of the terrain, the zero datum of the whole landscape. Now here on the riverboat, with my Koreans snapping their camera shutters like flamenco music as we cruised past St. Paul's in

close elevation, past Bankside, where the round wooden the-
aters stand in those first Dutch panoramas from a generation
before the great fire, I felt a similar exhilaration. I imagined a
sward of open land the same width as this river cutting
through the city on the other side of the cathedral, passing
through land that was bombed flat in 1940 and then built up
into Paternoster Square—now to be knocked flat again by demolition crews and built up in yet another version of the city,
with buildings looking like God knows what but having floors
deep enough and cooling coils powerful enough to cope with
computers. And why not? Because it could stay empty! The
city could have an internal panorama field, running clear
from Ludgate to the Bank of England, bounded on the north by
the Guildhall, with St. Paul's standing in the middle. It would
be a sight to revive Canaletto from his grave, paintbrushes
clasped between the digits of his skeleton. I have heard memories of the time immediately after the war, in the early 1950s,
when the bomb sites were still open land and the city still had
no tall buildings. The sites of the bombed-out buildings were
demolished down to basement level, with low walls around
them to stop people falling in—and on the thick layer of ash at
the bottom, wonderful self-seeded gardens bloomed. First it
was thistles and ragged robin, then nettles and columbine,
and then it all gradually turned into bramble thicket, like the
grounds of Sleeping Beauty's castle. Before too long the
clamor of building started, and the city slowly began filling up
again as a basin fills up with water, and, indeed, it still is filling up: so much so that we now have protected views of the
cities of London and Westminster from the tops of the surrounding hills so we can still see the genesis of the place and
not fall to wondering where in hell's name we are.

The hills of London are not like the seven hills of Rome. In Rome, the hills crowd in on the city, springing wells to supply water in those famous aqueducts and providing steep sides for defense. The London hills stand back from the city, providing recreation, a ground for fairs and looking at the horizon. They are not the climax of the city, like the Acropolis in Athens; nor is the view from the top a single perspective like that obtained from Montmarte when looking over Paris. The London hills are ranged on both sides of the city, north and south, and they gently rise to about three hundred feet above the river, over a distance of five miles. On a clear day—in spring or autumn, without the mist of winter or the haze of summer—you can stand at Alexandra Palace and see right across London to the mast of Crystal Palace, on a hill the same height ten miles away to the south, and then on beyond that another five miles to the Croydon Hills behind, at the edge of the Chalk Hills that form the London Basin.

From Parliament Hill, toward the western edge of the northern range, people with binoculars can watch airliners dropping behind the North Downs into Gatwick Airport, thirty miles away. From the same hill, as dusk approaches at the equinoxes, say at six o'clock in the evening, you can watch the planes queuing up to run in along the line of the Thames to Heathrow Airport off to the west. At this time of day, the navigation lights illuminate a dozen planes in the air at the same time, separated a couple of miles by air traffic control. This moving string of lights spans the whole city, each plane dropping its wheels in turn as it passes over

Gunnersbury, with seven miles of glide slope still to run; and under this stately, long-distance choreography, and from this vantage point, the whole ground, right out to Crystal Palace and beyond, is covered with the spangles of city lights. White and green in the buildings, yellow in the streets, with flashes of red from the cars and flashes of blue from the electric trains running along the edge of Hampstead Heath.

The London Basin is a syncline fold of chalk about forty miles across from tip to tip, from the North Downs to the Chilterns. Over the chalk, stretching from Croydon in the south to Elstree in the north, are beds of sands and clays, laid down in Tertiary times, just before the ice ages, and it is over these that the Thames meanders in its lower course, running from west to east along the center of the basin. Since the ice came and went, a series of flood plain terraces have been left behind as the land levels have changed relative to the sea. At around fifty feet above the present-day sea level is the terrace that forms the flat ground of Hyde Park and runs out through Bethnal Green to the Lee Valley: the edge of this is so close to the Thames at one point that St. Paul's, which is built on the terrace, seems to be standing on a hill by the river. That's why you look up at it from the riverboat. The terrace is called the Taplow. Further out, there is another terrace, called the Boyn Hill, about one hundred feet above sea level. This one has been heavily eroded: the wind-blasted hill of Pentonville, with its prison on top, is a remnant. The hills beyond this last terrace, about five miles from the Thames to both north and south, rise to one hundred meters,

St. Paul's Cathedral from Parliament Hill. Photograph by the author.

just over three hundred feet. They are not terraces but clay hills dragged by the glaciers and topped by sandy rocks, and it is from these—from Sydenham Hill and Forest Hill to the south, and from Muswell Hill and Parliament Hill to the north—that one looks back across the basin to the other side, clear across the river and its terraces and the buildings of London to the limit of the city's expansion in about the year 1900. Go further out, to Addenbrooke Hill outside Croydon or to the ridge east of Elstree, right on the edges of the clay, look back across the basin, and you can see the twentieth-century expansion of the city and the backs of the inner ranges of hills.

Seeing the whole of London takes some doing. There was a time when you could stand at Westminster and look downriver and see the city discrete inside its walls—but that time is long gone. My guess is that the Plantagenets were the last people really to have that whole view of the city. Now, you must try much harder. Cruising through the city on a riverboat is an appetizer, and there is always the air view if you can get the job as traffic spotter for the local radio, but to get a comprehensive view from the ground, to see what measure the place has taken on since Plantagenet times, requires a contour map, a bit of traveling, and that pair of binoculars.

It was in this mode that I strode up Parliament Hill one autumn day, to look at the horizon. In those early panoramas of London from Southwark Cathedral, like the one Thomas Wyck did in 1650, you can see the distant hill I was walking up in the background. *To paint hills in the distance,* says Leonardo in his color theory of depth, *the further away they are, add more blue.* There is a later painting by John Ritchie, made in the railway-building days of 1859, showing Sunday recreation on Hampstead Heath, with the city in the background. In Ritchie's painting there are fields as far as St. Pancras. You can just see the dome of St. Paul's lying against the hills on the other side, with its lantern and gilded cross sticking up into the sky. That's what I wanted to have a look at now. The day had started out breezy, but even as I left the house the wind was starting to get up, and by the time I reached the top of the hill the trees were thrashing about like children having nightmares, and the squirrels had left the branches and were cowering in the grass. Parliament Hill is a great place for horizon gazing and plane spotting, and for kite flying. In any sort of breeze there will be people with kites up there, from burly young men wrestling with stunt kites that can lift them off the ground to little children chasing after cotton lozenges with newspapers knotted into tails. On this blowy day, with my trousers flapping like the flag on a cross-channel ferry, I expected to find the place deserted, but no: someone was up there. A middle-aged man with a fisherman's beard and bright eyes and a sheepskin jacket was leaning into the wind like a Trojan, hanging on to the end of a kite-string spool with all his strength.

"Where is it?" I yelled at him, over the wind. I couldn't see the kite anywhere.

"Over there!" he yelled back, trying to point out the direction with his nose. "I daren't let go of this spool!" he said. "I paid out three thousand yards before this wind came up and it's a twelve-foot kite. It's pulling too hard for me to wind it in!"

Three thousand yards was way out over Finchley somewhere, getting on for two miles. The string was humming with the tension in it. It just disappeared into the sky if you looked at it, but I put my hand on it and I could feel the enormous strain. That's the joy of kite flying: feeling the power of the wind.

"It's all I can do to hang on to it," he shouted. "I should have known better. The last time I did this, the kite went shooting up vertically, right up into the air lanes. It showed up on radar at West Drayton, and the police came roaring up here in squad cars and made me pull it in. I couldn't pull it in now if they put a gun to my head!"

It was uncanny watching this invisible force working on the man, and I could see that it was starting to wear him out. In the end we devised an emergency plan. I put my arms around his waist and wrenched him backward against the wind, then let him go while he reeled in a couple of feet of line, then I wrenched him back again. Eventually the big kite came reluctantly into view, and we landed it and lay flat on our backs, completely drenched with the effort, trying to recover.

If you look straight ahead and hold your arms out perpendicular to your ears, you can't see your hands. But if you move them ever so slightly forward, a few degrees only, they will appear, right on the edge of your peripheral vision. A healthy human can see 170 degrees, still looking straight ahead. I tried it there on the grass, lying flat on my back. Fifteen yards to my right a shallow rise in the ground was glimmering like an air reconnaissance model of the Ural Mountains. It was a tiny horizon—which reminded me of what I had come up the hill to do. I stood up on my hind legs and brushed the bits of grass off myself and looked out to the south, across the city toward Crystal Palace.

The high winds had blown every scrap of haze out of the sky. I have never seen it so clear, before or since. The distant hills were not blue but a rich russet brown. I scanned through my binoculars, and I could make out the fine detail of the city—Ludgate, Holborn, Cheapside, King's Cross. I thought of those angry poems by William Blake in which the Old Testament is played out against the names of London as though it were the holy battleground. Then I turned my gaze on St. Paul's and noticed for the first time that the tip of the dome coincided exactly with the horizon of the far hills. I was looking clear across the city from one side to the other, with St. Paul's bang in the middle, and I saw that the tip of the dome of the cathedral brushes the horizon—and the lantern on top sticks up into the sky.

In the past, when I would look from this hill through the binoculars I would see the ant-size tourists cramming the viewing gallery on the tip of the dome—with their feet, I now realized, at the same level as my feet on this hill—and I would imagine them signaling to me with an Aldis lamp, *Twenty-Twenty!* or some such thing, *Deutschland über Alles!* But now that I had seen this coincidence of the horizon and the tip of the dome, the rest of my day was a foregone conclusion. I raced off down the hill, got into the car, and set off for the other side of London. Down past Nelson's Column and Whitehall, across the river at Lambeth, via Elephant and Castle to Dulwich, and up onto the hill at Crystal Palace. The view from there, alas, was obscured by trees, so I traced the line of the southern ridge back through Sydenham and to the Horniman Gardens on Forest Hill, all the time trying to see St. Paul's through the trees. At last, on a hilltop road of little white houses built of cheap bricks and concrete tiles, I found what I was looking for: the dome of St. Paul's seen against the hills I had started from, ten miles away to the north.

The view was worth waiting for. It is not a protected view, although it should be, it's important enough: the tip of the dome clips the horizon and the lantern on top sticks up into the sky. St. Paul's Cathedral is the same height as the hills on either side. It fills up the basin as the city does. St. Paul's is the touchstone for the whole city. I was so excited that I accosted the first person I saw—a woman with two little dogs who played in the gutters like a pair of delinquent children— and she was not all that interested. I told her anyway. It was as exciting to me as the discovery of Tutankhamen's tomb must have been to Flinders Petrie. I thought I had found the logic of the settlement of the London Basin. I went home and checked the textbooks: total height of St. Paul's, 366 feet. Subtract the height of the lantern that sticks above the horizon, 88 feet, which gives a height to the top of the dome of 278 feet. Add the height of the pavement above sea level, 50 feet, and you get a total of 328 feet above sea level: exactly one hundred meters, the same height as Parliament Hill and Crystal Palace.

———

The St. Paul's I had been concentrating on was built in 1712 to replace the old Gothic church that was destroyed in the Fire of London. Until the English Civil War, the old church was always full of people. London was a densely packed jumble of stuff, and the only public spaces were out on the edge. There was Tower Hill, where they executed people; there was Smithfield, where they had markets and fairs; and there was Moorfields, where they practiced sports. But there was also St. Paul's. The church and its churchyard were the crossroads of the city. Gathering to pray was a tiny part of it. The church was always open. People used the transept as a shortcut from north to south; they lounged and talked and traded in the nave; they left notes for each other tacked on the doors. It was as much a public gardens as it was a church.

This unpious commerce was cleared out by Oliver Cromwell. I imagine the church after the visitation of Puritan axemen: statues beheaded, silver purloined, the whole thing looking like the austere Protestant churches in the Holland of that time. The building has been painted white and emptied of everything but the pulpit. On the walls hang a few hatchments, the lozenge-shaped coats of arms of dead worthies. No statues, no money lending, no lounging, no gossip. Nothing.

Six years after the end of the Commonwealth, the building was burned down by the Great Fire, and 50 years later still, there stood the new church, the one we see today, in the same place. Not exactly the same place: the plan was slewed around a little bit counterclockwise and moved a little to the east to separate the foundations of the new from the foundations of the old. Now it is another 280 years later, and the commerce and the lounging of the sixteenth century are back. The place is teeming with foot traffic and the sound of cash registers. The people are tourists, and the commerce is souvenirs. People stand in long lines to get in, and when in, with the great specter of the interior before them, are immediately diverted through a turnstile past a cash register. The west end of the nave has two cash registers, a donations casket, a stand holding taped tours of the cathedral in several languages, the main postcard and souvenir desk, and another stall run by tho Frionds of St. Paul's selling St. Paulian memorabilla. The place is filling up with this stuff as the city outside is filling up with rentable office space. In front of the crypt staircase on the south transept is a kiosk of postcards and film, and halfway down the south aisle is a bookstore. There is another ticket desk at the entrance to the dome staircase.

"Boy," I say to the man sitting behind it, "you could write an anthem for the cash registers in this place!"

"Have you visited your exhibition in the choir?" he says. "It's about the connection between the House of Windsor and St. Paul's. And in the crypt restaurant today we are serving summer pudding."

He is a curate. He is dressed in one of those long black dresses with a high collar and cloth-covered buttons all the way up the front. What is going on? "One ticket for the dome? Take the stairs and keep to the right, please." *Ding!* and the drawer full of cash slides out and nudges him in the belly.

I have come here to climb up to the Golden Gallery at the top of the dome and look out at the hills I have been looking in from. It is the end of the season, cheap travel time, and school parties are bussing in from the Continent, schoolchildren packing the ferries like veal calves. The stair to the dome is thronged with teenagers, as flirtatious as chaffinches in the spring. On the way up, I stop off at the Whispering Gallery, which runs around the inside of the dome at the same height as the top of the nave. It's called the Whispering Gallery because you can bounce messages around the walls to your friends a hundred feet away, and it sounds as though you are whispering in their ears. It's perfect for flirting. Over the giggles and whispers comes the sound of the Lord's Prayer. *Our Father, who art in Heaven,* comes drifting up from the pulpit, so corrupted with echoes in the complex soundpit of the cathedral that I can identify it only by the cadence of the chant.

St. Paul's is only three-quarters the size of St. Peter's in Rome, but it has a dome far more ingenious than Michelangelo's. The lantern at the top is held up by a brick cone, but there is an inner dome as well, pierced at the eye, which gives the spectators, glued to the transept floor with their necks bent back double, a view clear up past the inner dome and into an allegory of heavenly order painted on the inside of the cone. The lead dome visible from the hills is propped from the outside of the cone by big oak struts. To reach the gallery, you clamber up a spiral iron stair that cuts back and forth between the struts as the profile of the dome closes in toward the top. Today, this strange interstitial space is filled with the cries of teenage tourists, and there is plenty of vertigo to elicit those cries. About halfway up I come across a French girl in turquoise dungarees and pink Reeboks hyperventilating with terror, frozen to the spot while her three friends stroke her back and try to soothe her. All she can think of is that she still has to get back down to earth. I stop to see if I can help but succeed only in frightening her friends, so I push on past them. On the next landing, some German boys are enjoying cigarettes out of sight of their teacher. Now, I am not a puritan, but we are 250 feet up a 280-year-old structure: the whole thing could catch fire as fast as a Los Angeles canyon. When I wave my hand to say *No Smoking! Verboten!* the one holding the cigarette looks at me like a prisoner and flicks the glowing stub down into the depths of the construction. The way down is blocked by the throng of people coming up. I cross my fingers and climb on up toward the viewing gallery.

You can see everything from up there. You can see the whole of London, from Harrow to Dartford, from Barnet to Croydon. With the sun behind it, the radio mast at Crystal Palace seems close enough to touch; on the other side, there are the office blocks of Barnet twenty miles away, in the hollow between Alexandra Palace and Muswell Hill. The gallery is in the open and runs right around the tip of the dome, but it is only two feet wide, and it is party time—there must be forty people up here. Our jostling feet are on a level with the hills to north and south, and our backs are up against the white stone lantern, its baroque edges all softened by erosion. It weighs nine hundred tons, that lantern, as much as four jumbo jets: if you made a lantern out of jumbo jets standing on their tails, they would stick up above the horizon almost as far as the distance from here to the ground.

Once back down on the black-and-white floor of the cathedral, I reflect on the clearing away of clutter. In the city at large, the Great Fire has done it; the blitz has done it; it could be done again. Inside the building, Cromwell did it, and it could be done again. Out go the kiosks, the cash registers, the signs saying this and that. Out go the stack of chairs and temporary staging that they store in the south transept where the font used to be, and which obscures the statue of Lieutenant General Sir Ralph Abercromby. He died fighting Napoleon in Egypt in 1801, and his memorial inscription contains two sentences, each of them more than one hundred words long. The white marble statue shows Sir Ralph in the arms of the angels of mercy. Nineteen such statues of the Napoleonic War heros are distributed around the cathedral, all erected in the huge gush of relief that followed the victory at Waterloo. But why should they be here? And why should the Middlesex regiment fill up the north transept with its maudlin little memorials? I have seen a painting of the cathedral by Thomas Malton, circa 1790, before these statues were erected, when it was completely empty. So out with the chairs, and out with the chandeliers, and out with all the statues, too! We could set them all up in the new panorama field, when all the garbage outside gets cleared out as well. A plan for St. Paul's is a plan for the city, too. It's a landscape strategy, and it's called *vision*. It means seeing everything as far as you can see.

THE BASIN

"I'll drive the bus," says Adam, speaking in his businesslike mode, which could at any moment turn into silly-ass mode, "but I want Eve to sit next to me." It is a huge joke for everyone that Adam goes out with Eve. The coincidence of their names is what has kept them together through Adam's drunken lurchings and retchings and Eve's tight-lipped affairs with other men.

"It'll wear you out," I tell him. The whole circuit around outer London is eighty miles. It'll take from dawn to dusk even though this is the longest day of the year.

"I am made of steel," says Adam. "I never wear out."

He is one of thirteen students who are climbing on board a bus with me and setting off for a photographic reconnaissance of the horizon seen from the outlying hills—the hills that lie another seven miles beyond Parliament Hill and Crystal Palace, out on the perimeter of the London Basin. All the students have telephoto lenses, which is good news, because we will be traveling at a twelve-mile radius from St. Paul's, which is serving as the locus of concentration, and a standard lens is undiscriminating at that distance. My own lens is 200 mm, magnification 4x. Eve's friend Julie has a big white Nikon 1000 mm and a heavy-duty tripod to go with it. Eve and Julie are both slight women, by which I mean that they eat nothing but avocado pears, strawberries, and crisp-bread in order not to bulge out of their tight black leather coats. It takes both of them to heave the tripod and the lens onto the bus.

Today, it is a special treat to have Sally with us. She has broken with Shahriar, because, she says, he was only pre-tending that he thought women and men existed on the same plane.

"But he worshiped you!" I was surprised. I thought they were in it for the duration.

"Isn't that what I just said?" She looked at me and reached across and pulled my collar straight. "He started to say I was his Artemis! Ridiculous! I felt more like a field he was ploughing."

"Shah did always love the land," I grinned. I was thinking of the Aurthurian legend. "You know, *the king and the land are one.*"

"Well, I'm a woman," said Sally. "I'm not a landscape." *Tell me about it!* "Even when we were walking side by side he thought he was three paces in front of me."

She installed herself in the front seat next to Eve, so it was left to Asif, his face pockmarked like the surface of Pluto, to occupy the seat next to me.

"Why come all the way to England to study landscape when you have the Pyramids to look at at home?" I asked him when we first met.

"My father is an enemy of the president. We had to leave."

"As soon as you get a chance, go and look at the white cliffs at Beachy Head." He got his notebook and wrote it down. "If you're going to live here, you might as well start at

The top of the Canary Wharf tower sticking up above the horizon of the Hampstead hills, seen from Elstree, England. Photograph by the author.

the beginning." That's where, on a clear day, you can see the coast of France clear across the Channel.

We are all aboard. Adam climbs into the driver's seat and turns the vehicle around in one lazy circle, bumping over the sidewalks on both sides, and makes off up the road, experimenting with the gears. Before too long we have hit the main road and have picked up some speed. I love this mode of travel. Buses are such steady vehicles. Sitting on a bus on the open road is like time passing, like aging. Young people on long bus journeys mature as cheeses do, just sitting there on the shelves. The road is full of enormous trucks pulling produce in and out of London, and overhead the airliners are banking and turning as they take off from Heathrow.

Alex, sitting in front of me, is the most thoughtful of all the students. He reads Burroughs and listens to Berio, and like a macrobiotic who is *careful about what he eats,* Alex is careful about what he thinks. He turns to me and says, "This is what a city is, these big infrastructures. Reservoirs, motorways, airports. The things in the middle, the office blocks and churches, they're like the parking meters. Small change." It's Alex's politics: privilege is small change compared to the vigorous might of the modern world. It's not cities that are obsolete, it's city centers.

"Wait until you see the whole thing from up on Harrow Hill," I tell him. "Then decide what the whole thing is."

Our first stop is at Runnymede, where the roof of the air force memorial gives a spectacular view of the western half of London. The building is perched on the edge of a wooded cliff above the Thames, where the beds of sand that make up the inner hills coalesce into the much bigger mass of the Bagshot Beds, which fill up the west end of the basin. You reach the roof up a secret stair and through a copper-and-glass cupola, and everyone is noisily exhilarated by the view. Julie calls it *searing.* The city itself is obscured by the hump of Richmond Park, but we can see the Highgate Hills to the north, covered with trees, and the church spire on top of Harrow Hill, which marks the inswinging western boundary of the inner hills. Below us, spread out on the flood plain, are the reservoirs and the airport. We are at about nine o'clock on the circle.

Alex sidles up to me, pushes the hair out of his face, and says in a low voice, "I reckon this is cheating. We're up on a building here; if we want to see this basin thing, we should be standing on the proper ground. We might as well go up a tower block as stand here." That's exactly what I think. The only buildings that play a part in this investigation are those with an exact height and an explicit relation to the basin. My colleague in demolition theory Michael Gold has pointed out how Silbury Hill in Wiltshire is the same height as its surrounding horizon, too. It's part of the Stonehenge and White Horse and Long Kennet complex of horizon-oriented things from Neolithic times. Years ago an excavation was made to see what Silbury Hill was for. There were no skeletons inside, so the scholars left the site, mystified, but what they found is perfectly clear, if you look at the section: an earth mound, *faced with chalk boulders* and then covered with turf. It is among chalk hills—it is the same height as the hills around it—it is an imitation hill. But is it, because it is made by humans, a building, like a tower block? Or is it a landscape, like the "proper ground," as Alex calls it? We all go back down to the parking lot and get back in the bus. Asif pulls out a sandwich and starts eating it, but he's the only one who doesn't realize how uncool food is. The rest of them are having cigarettes for lunch. We set off for Harrow Hill in a haze of blue smoke.

A phone rings. Sally feels around in her bag and extracts a small Motorola. We all prick up our ears and listen to Sally give a demonstration of how to fend off yet another entreaty from your devastated ex-lover.

"I know it's difficult," she says. "It's hard for me, too. But you want my advice?" There is a pause, and we can just hear the groans of a caged beast coming from the other end.

"Listen, Shah—"

"Oh, how it hurts when you say my name!"

"*Listen,* Shah. Do what I'm doing. Get used to it!"

She snaps the mouthpiece shut in the mobile equivalent of slamming the receiver down. She turns to face her audience: we are bouncing up and down in our seats in unison, our eyes wide and our ears flapping, like a nest full of owlets.

"You want my advice? Get used to it!" she says, and laughs in a way that, if he heard it, would make Shahriar disintegrate.

––––––––

Harrow is another hundred-meter hill, a dozen miles as the crow flies to the dome of St. Paul's. The church spire is the main horizon landmark of the western edge, but the view toward the city to the east is the preserve of Harrow School. To get our photographs, we will have to go trespassing. To encourage the students in this deed, I tell them of one of the lesser-known traditions of this bastion of privilege. When they leave, the Harrow School boys give each other playing-card-size photographs of themselves, so they all have a pack of their peers to help them in playing the game of *old boy's jungle.* They dress up for these photos in tight leathers and shades, fishnet tights, lipstick, you name it. They explain the practice to themselves by saying that Byron went to Harrow, and his brand of reckless romanticism has left its mark. I am making it all up, of course—but we, too, Byronically climb the wall onto the east terrace. It's worth it—it's one of the best long-distance panoramas of London there is. We are looking down the center of the basin toward the sea now, and at this distance the dome of St. Paul's is a tiny blip. Among the general clutter, however, three high buildings stand out: Canary Wharf, the NatWest Building, and the Telecom Tower.

At that moment Asif appears, shouting excitedly. He has taken my binoculars up to the other side of the church, looking out toward the west, and has discovered that he can see another Telecom mast, the one that stands on the edge of the Chiltern Hills where the motorway cuts through the chalk scarp on its way to Oxford. That's forty miles away. There is a mass exodus up to the churchyard to check this out, and pretty soon it is established that at least another two Telecom towers are visible, way out to the south. It is a fine way to illustrate that the height of the Telecom Tower is as critical as the height of St. Paul's: still related to the height of the hills of the basin, but in a different way. It has to be higher than they are to broadcast its radio waves over the hills to the other masts that grid the country.

It is no accident that our attention has been diverted from the phenomenon of St. Paul's being the same height as the hills around to the fact of these other tall buildings in the city. I have planned it this way. The next stop, at Elstree, due north of St. Paul's and still twelve miles out, will prove it. The time has come to get back in the bus and move on, but we have lost Eve. Adam goes looking for her and locates her sitting on Angelica Byron's grave, in the churchyard, lost in thought. He leads her back to the bus and hands her into the front seat, ironically, as though he were a gentleman.

"I've been thinking about knowledge and experience," she says. Imagine her sitting on the front seat in her flowered skirt and her leather jacket and her long curtains of black hair, white faced, thin as a stake, twisting around and lecturing the rest of us on the matter. She says that ever since she was seven years old and read about what Eve did in Genesis, she has wanted answers to some questions.

"In the first place, why did Adam bother to name all the animals? There weren't any other humans then, so what did he need language for? It can't have been to think with—he was in paradise, and who needs reason in paradise? So what did he do it for?"

Sally says it is a curriculum, a preordained knowledge. But this is Eve's point: "There is no knowledge without experience—that's why you've brought us up here, isn't it? You couldn't just tell us about the London Basin, we have to feel it, don't we?"

She's right.

"You have to eat the apple, don't you?"

At this, the rest of the bus is starting to groan, not sharing Eve's vested interest in the question. She shuts up, looking miserable.

Sally says, "If she hadn't given the apple to Adam he'd never have realized they could be having sex! Besides," she went on, stroking the rumpled Eve on the arm, "it wasn't eating the apple that was sinful, it was the disobedience." We all agree that reason is the enemy of obedience—and I am delighted to be in this bus with fourteen inheritors of the thirst for experience. It is just one vehicle traveling through a world still smothered in curriculums, a world where people adhere to conventions and can't see the wood for the trees. In my version, that's *can't see the ground for the buildings*—and so I'm showing this bunch the ground.

We are back on the highway now, and everyone is half asleep. To keep awake, Adam is telling Sally about a recent injustice inflicted on him. He said he had an idea to make a building with a huge blank red wall as a facade, and he was torn into by his critics.

"That's not an idea!" they said. "You can't call that an idea. What's to discuss in it? How does it help the world? F minus!" Sally said she agreed with them.

Huh?

"Of course it's not an idea. It's a vision."

"Painting a wall red is a vision?" says Adam.

"It's rudimentary, but it's still a vision. You're on the right track. Your teachers explain and explain all the time, and come up with ideas and discuss what to do with them, and what changes? Nothing changes! Landscape's too big a subject for ideas. It needs visions." She revolves in her seat and looks at me. "The vision itself doesn't have to be a big thing— look at your panorama field at St. Paul's. You have to see it to propose it. No amount of explanation can justify it."

It is midday, and we have reached Elstree. Twelve o'clock on the circle. A tiny road barely wide enough for the bus runs through some trees and stops at the edge of the hill, looking south. The tail of the motorway swings to the east across the hill below us, making for the Edgware junction. We are 450 feet above sea level, looking across the Hampstead ridge toward London, which is hidden from view. All you can see of the city are the three towers, Canary Wharf, NatWest, and

British Telecom, sticking up above the hill. We have fourteen photographs to prove it. The Telecom tower peeps over the hill to broadcast over it. Canary Wharf and the NatWest tower are higher than the hill for a less fundamental, but possibly as profound, reason—they are both striving to be the tallest building in the patch.

"In that case," says Alex, "Canary Wharf has won. The black one's obsolete. They should demolish it."

"Or build a higher one still and demolish Canary Wharf," says Adam. Is the boy a prophet? Or has Sally's flattery gone to his head? He says the Sears Building is nearly twice as high, 1,450 feet, and we stand and look. For a moment we are all visionaries. We imagine it built there, on the other side of the hill, towering into the sky.

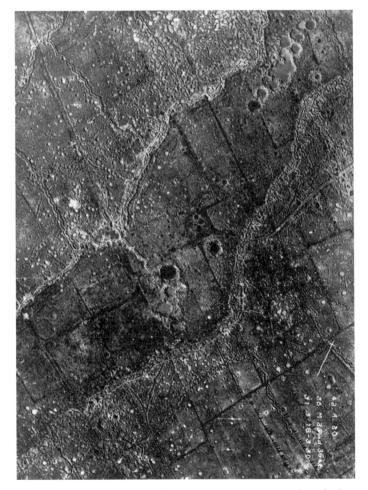

A vertical aerial view of German and British trenches facing each other at Neuve Chapelle, France, March 1918. Courtesy Imperial War Museum, London, Q45960.

7

MEMORY

THE WESTERN FRONT

*How long is forever? This is a difficult question. How long is a day? Easy.
There are 365¼ days in a year and 365,250 in a millennium. Since the
earliest recorded human civilization in Jericho, 9000 B.C., there have been
just over 4 million days. Is that a lot or a little?*

—————————— BATTLESCAPE ——————————

Gertrude Stein is the one who wrote that curious line *A rose is a rose is a rose is a rose.* She explained much later that when the language was new, in Chaucer's day, a poet could write a single word and fill the reader with emotion, but now that the language was centuries old, steeped in use—now that our ears were dulled—the structural requirements of poetry had become more exacting.

"I am no fool," she said, "but I think that in that line the rose is red for the first time in English poetry for a hundred years."

A rose is a rose is a rose is a rose is a modernist's repetition. It is not the classical flashing of galley oars in sea-soaked sunlight; it is machine-made repetition, continuously spooling off the end of the belt. No sweat, no tears, just plenty for all. The modernists loved the machines so much that the repetition of components became in the end the very figure of modernism; but allow me to point you in this other direction, over here, in this concrete dugout. For a piece of mechanistic feedback loop repetition, what better example is there than the machine gun? A bang is a bang is a bang is a bang! Six hundred times a minute!

Stein and her friend, Alice Toklas, volunteered to work for the American Fund for the French Wounded in 1917,

Men of the Sixteenth Canadian Machine Gun Company, Fourth Division, on Passchendaele Ridge, Belgium, November 1917. Courtesy Imperial War Museum, London, C02246.

which was the third year of World War I. They lived in Paris but had been in London during the outbreak of war in the autumn of 1914. Stein told people there that she knew the Germans would not win. When the English furrowed their brows and emanated their genteel disquiet that the Germans were so *organized*, she roared at them, "Can't you see the difference between organization and method?" She said the Germans were not a modern people: "Any two americans, any twenty americans, any millions of americans can organize themselves to do something, but not the germans." She said the Germans were *medieval,* that they could formulate a method, and they could have a method put upon them, but they could never organize. That is why they would not win the war.

Well, here's one method. Here's what you do with your dead soldiers. You gather all the bodies together and strip them naked, and package up their clothes and effects with a label bearing their number. You take the corpses and arrange them heads to feet in bunches of four and bind them together with industrial wire, around their necks and ankles and waists. The rigor mortis will keep them in order. You dispatch them for burial to the homeland stacked five bunches deep in railway wagons. Is that not methodical? Or is it just anti-German propaganda, a rumor spread by the French inhabitants of occupied France? The conditions of the Western Front were so severe that it could be true. The horror would be just one of many.

"A landscape is such a natural setting for a battle or a play," continued the marvelous Stein, "that one must write plays." Shakespeare's *Henry the Fifth* is both: a play about the battle of Agincourt. The French spell it *Azincourt.* It was the climax of the Hundred Years' War between England and France and ended in a victory, against the odds, for King Henry. I imagine him processing through the streets of Dover on his return and up the Old Kent Road with his new French wife—his alliance—beside him, with his face painted bright red in imitation of a triumphant Roman emperor. *Here comes the Renaissance!*

The prologue of Shakespeare's play is an apology for its lack of action, compared with the great events it represents;

an apology for its little domain, the theater building, compared with the vast fields of France; an apology for its short duration, which compresses the accomplishments of many years into an hour or two. But if six zeros in a row can represent a million on a piece of paper, a bunch of actors can represent the whole human race on a stage. You can imagine the king's players acting out the physical realities of Azincourt on the stage of the Globe theatre; the heavy rain that preceded it, which caused the mud that enmired the battlefield; the way the English archers stuck their feet into the mud to steady themselves—it was St. Crispin the Bootmaker's day— and the way the French cavalry charge lost all its momentum in the mire. You can imagine the counting of the dead after the battle, and the gathering of the bodies.

Old soldiers have a vision of every battle as part of some great war that has been going on since humans began. Some pieces of the landscape are so perfect for battle that they have been chosen over and over again, they say, and one of these is the shoulder of northwest France. The mud and massacre that framed the battle of Azincourt is too like the battle of the Somme to deny the old soldiers' delusion. That is why one must write plays.

All through World War I, as the number of casualties increased and the lists of the dead spooled out of the battlefields like machinery, the London *Times* published a map showing the current state of the Western Front. Three tiny villages, which would otherwise not be included on a map of this scale, are carefully marked: Azincourt, Crécy, and Waterloo. Three ancient British victories, to encourage another to happen.

As pre-battle pep talks go, that map is a somber little gesture. Grand exhortations like the one Shakespeare had Henry give before his pretend Azincourt are not easy things to construct, and perhaps only Shakespeare could do it—if you read *Henry the Fifth,* act 4, scene 3, lines 20 to 67, you will see what I mean—but what a project that would be: to be the twentieth century's Shakespeare and write the Western Front as a five-act verse drama. It could be called *XIV–XVIII.* Wilfred Owen's voice would be played by the same man who plays the melancholy Jaques in *As You Like It.* The generals would be not so much obstinate donkeys as human beings caught in a time confusion; and what words would be given to General Foch, supreme Allied commander, on realizing that the Russian Revolution has closed the *Eastern* Front and released 2 million Germans to reinforce the Western Front, thus making their spring 1918 offensive possible? The Americans were starting to appear in the field just then, and it was something of a race for time by the German high command before a flood of doughboys canceled out their reinforcements; so let's jump genres. Let's have Foch say, "Wait until you see the whites of their eyes, boys." His ploy worked. They waited, the attack ran out of steam, and six months later, after a four-year stalemant, the Germans had been driven out of France.

After the war was over, the French looked up and found almost all of their country untouched. Almost all—the war had been fought with such intensity over such a small area of ground that the Western Front remined distinct for several years. A blur of churned-up ground, only a few miles wide, whose few remaining trees were decimated to stumps, pock-marked with craters, full of rusted metal and debris and un-exploded shells and the corpses of 4 million men, ran clear across France for 450 miles, from the English Channel all the way to the Alps. The seeds of poppy and charlock can stay underground for many years until some upheaval brings them to the surface and they burst into flower. A high-explosive bombardment is just right for it. That is why in the summer after the war this devastated stripe of ground blazed red and yellow, *blood and bandages,* bringing the concentrated time of war and the timelessness of the wilderness into one picture.

The Germans had first invaded France in the autumn of 1914, repulsing the French and British counterattacks and pushing their opposition back until they were at last stopped on the line of the river Marne, only twenty miles from Paris. Their attempt to outflank the British to the Channel was un-successful, but the holding operation took three months, and by December the line of the Western Front, with 5 million men entrenched and facing each other across a small strip of no-man's-land, was established. The whole of the next twelve months was taken up with fruitless French and British attempts to push the Germans back. At the beginning of the next year the Germans mounted a huge attack on the French stonghold of Verdun, more or less in the middle of the line; the battle went on continually from February to November. The big British offensive to the west, around the

Somme, was an attempt to break the Germans even as they were attempting to break the French at Verdun. Neither plan worked, but colossal casualties resulted on both sides. In the winter of that year the Germans fortified their rear lines from Arras to Soissons, the Hindenburg Line, and fell back to a defensive position. Nineteen seventeen saw big French offensives to the east of the Hindenburg Line, and British offensives to the west: both were held by the Germans, and the exhausted French and British armies almost dissolved in mutiny—but by then the United States was in the fight. There was an intimation of future success for the British at the end of the year when tanks were used at Cambrai to break the Hindenburg Line temporarily. At that moment, the Russian Revolution shut the Eastern Front down, and a great influx of Germans from the east enabled them to mount a big offensive in the spring of 1918, using shock tactics developed in Russia. The attack ran out of momentum after the Germans had forced three salients in the line some thirty miles deep, and with the huge advantage of fresh American troops now in place, the counteroffensive over the summer ended the stalemate of the trench lines for good and pushed the Germans right out of France by the start of the winter. The cease-fire was signed in November after just over four years of fighting.

The battered strip of land over which this long war of attrition was fought has since been rescued and restored. Villages have been rebuilt, woods replanted, craters and trenches filled in, farming resumed, the dead bodies buried in marked graves whenever possible. A dozen miles on either side of the line, the old French landscape is as it always was—but along the line itself, which was reduced by battery to muddy nothing, it is as though the landscape has suffered a calamitous compression, has been passed through a tiny eye and reinflated, slightly different from the rest.

The ruination of the landscape came from artillery fire. Every attack was preceded by a bombardment designed to destroy the other side's defenses, and then the attacks took place in the face of returning shell fire that made the no-man's-land that had to be crossed into a tossing storm of earth and blast and splinters of metal. More people were killed by shell fire than by the machine guns. Sometimes the shells came down so fast they couldn't be counted apart, as fast as teeth chattering. Every tree was reduced to a stump; every building was destroyed. Whole villages vanished and could be located only by the stain of brick dust mixed in the mud, or perhaps by a hungry dog, loitering in what had once been its own little patch. All this savage battery was added to by the activities of millions of men digging trenches, where they could at least be safe from flying bullets. At every tiny advance, perhaps five hundred yards gained after a week of heavy fighting, new trenches were dug to consolidate the position, with new secondary and tertiary trenches in support, and new communication trenches joining them together, all zigzagging across the ground in chevrons eight feet wide to eliminate the possibility of an enemy gun's raking down the line. Not only were they the most extensive earth defenses ever seen, but they were, within the confines of the Western

Front's sliver of strife, continuously changing and being abandoned and rebuilt. Mixed up in all this movement of the earth, the blast of shells and the digging of trenches, was another movement—the burial of the dead. All along the line, corpses were interred in vaulting numbers, hundreds of thousands of them in battlefield graves, singly, in twos and threes, in platoon-sized bunches of 24, in company-sized clumps of 120, and even, in the worst days of the Somme, in battalion-sized masses of 600.

Now almost all this earthly turmoil has been restored. Occasionally a piece of woodland still shows ground spattered with craters under the trees. In one or two places, such as the park created in memory of the Canadians who died fighting to take Beaumont Hamel in the battle for the Schwaben redoubt in the summer of 1916, the ground has been kept as it was, trenches and all, and dotted with monuments bearing lists of names of the dead. Mostly, however, the fields have been leveled and brought back under the plough, and the villages have been rebuilt, and the bodies that had not been disintegrated by the shelling have been marshaled into cemeteries of a couple hundred graves. Everywhere there are monuments to the fallen, too, stone statues of angels cradling French soldiers, or obelisks bearing epitaphs local to Yorkshire, or bronze statues of kilted highlanders carrying guns. In the places where the fighting was most intense, as at Ypres, or along the busy little road from Béthune to Armentières, or west of Lille, or on the Somme, the landscape is so full of memorials, so full of this postwar reconstruction, so full of the traces of the war in the remains of trenchworks and mine craters, that the landscape is still thick with the memory of that time.

The reconstruction of the landscape took place in the 1920s, when the long neoclassical period in building was stuttering to a halt and modern things were being produced amid clouds of argument, and that confusion, together with the depredations of the inflation that followed the war, have produced as dour a set of settlements as you will ever see. At a distance, all is fine. Around the valley of the Ancre, which was the British Somme battlefront, the villages are spread out over the rolling chalk landscape at intervals of two or three miles, so that from any one you will see two or three others, marked by their slated church spires on the horizon. Close up, however, these churches look like job lots, fussy brick impersonations of the landmarks they were built to replace.

If you stand on the line of the front as it was in July 1916 between Serre and Beaumont-Hamel, you can see the British cemeteries tracing the line, spaced a few hundred yards apart, their white crosses carrying your eye to the horizon. You can see the rebuilt church spires in the distance, see hillocks of ground where trenches once were, and feel the theme of memory upon you. One hundred miles to the south, Disneyland-Paris spreads itself across a piece of ground chosen for its commercial purpose. There is not much difference in the workings of each of these places on your understanding. To see either one clearly, it helps to know the narrative that goes with it. The difference is that in one, that narrative is Mickey Mouse—a banal folly. In the other, it's life and death, and a folly of a much huger kind.

At least 4 million men were killed along the strip of land that made the Western Front in those five years. The majority of them were killed by the shell fire. You were lucky if you were knocked out by the blast itself; most were killed by chunks of the metal case of the shell tearing into their flesh, and most of the dead were around twenty years old. My research assistant, Gareth, is twenty, too. He's a neat young man and follows Kurt Vonnegut's recipe for popularity—wear nice clothes, smile a lot, and know the words to the latest tunes—but that does not stop him from being a bit unsure of himself. He holds his opinions as he used to hold his toy guns as a child. He thinks, for example, that the bodies of people over forty are too full of bone to flex—ossified—and not still fresh, like his. Once, when I was stumbling over some half-remembered item, he declared that everything that's happened to him is still fresh to him. He told me about the time two years ago when he was traveling across the United States in a bus, in the months between high school and college. He has a photo album of the trip titled "Interstate Forty." In Arizona the bus driver was persuaded to divert to the Grand Canyon by a unanimous vote of passengers. The vote was organized by three girls who had set up a sort of blanket camp on the back seat of the bus, and Gareth, exhausted by his attempts to infiltrate this camp, was fast asleep by the time they got there. No one woke him—who would wake a sleeping baby?—and so he missed it. They showed him Polaroids afterward, but it wasn't the same. All the rest of the way to the Pacific Coast he was the butt of the joke.

The Thiepval Arch from the Albert-Bapaume road, south of Pozières, France. Photograph by the author.

"Hey Gareth, wake up! We're passing a Texaco station!"

In San Francisco his contact was a venerated architect, a friend of his mother's, who was famous for orchestrating temporary driftwood villages down there on the beach at Grey Whale Cove. He was a man well into his fifties, with a tan and a grizzled beard, who disarmed Gareth by saying on the phone, "Gareth! Great to hear from you, buddy! Come on over! I love talking to young folks—keeps me fresh!"

So on over he went, and he sat in an Eames chair next to a window the size of a cinema screen with the ocean outside as blue as technicolor, drinking lemonade, talking in his not-too-sure-of-himself way about the future. It was less than ten minutes before his host was fuming, pulling rank, calling him a brat and saying, "When you get to my age, buddy, you'll know different." Adding things like, "You wait till you've been in battle, boy, you won't be so cocky then."

But young men are cocky—that's why old men use them to fight wars. Young men don't recognize their mortality, they don't understand the discretion-and-valor thing, they don't get out of breath, they heal quickly, they have no children to live for, and when they're confused, they do what you tell them—they're perfect. And most of them love guns, like Gareth. He grew up watching soap operas with his sister, he clutching his plastic M-16, she sucking her thumb and clutching her Disco Barbie.

I first met Gareth during the Gulf War, and he used to fantasize about high-explosive landscapes. He videotaped every news report, showing the smart bombs inserting themselves through vent shafts and the cruise missiles following their little internal software street maps around Baghdad like dumb tourists. When I talked to him about demolition, he developed a whole landscape idea of high-precision explosive earthworks, saying you could make parks by attacking city blocks with smart bombs, taking them out in one event and reducing them to rubble.

"What, parks full of rubble? Who wants that?"

"Think about it! What a place for kids to play! Buildings reduced to dense matter, like the quarries and claypits they once were, and everything in them buried, waiting to be found, like Treasure Island!"

He is also interested in the landscaping possibilities of Star Wars. He described in tones of wonder the little missiles to be sent against incoming ballistics. They would be not high explosive but inert, like rocket-propelled slingshots.

They were called *Smart Rocks.* The following generation were to be smaller, faster, and more flexible in response; they were called *Brilliant Pebbles.* None of this has come to pass: the disintegration of the Evil Empire has forced the Ballistic Missile Defense Organization to change its mission in order to stay in existence. Now it is concentrating on the possibility of destroying asteroids passing dangerously close to the earth, with a program called REAACT: Rendezvous with Earth Approaching Asteroids and Comets. It is the new catastrophism. I pointed out to Gareth that these asteroids are solid lumps of rock maybe three or four miles across; they're not going to fragment when struck with a pebble, however brilliant it is.

"Okay, but it would make a great video game."

It has been observed that computerized war games are the only way to exercise a fight escalating all the way up to nuclear. This is because human war gamers hesitate to push the doomsday button, whereas machines don't skip a beat. The use of computers by the Pentagon war gamers has influenced the kind of weapons control that soldiers now use on real-time battlefields; consequently they treat it all as virtual reality. It makes a great video game.

I try and interest Gareth in the peaceful study of landscape by showing him the venerable J. B. Jackson's—John Jackson's—studies of rural America. The shape of liberal politics on the ground. I tell him about the town-and-country guarantees that William Penn built into the plan of Philadelphia, where the suburbs were interposed to stop the Tory-Whig acrimony that ruined England from reappearing in the colony. I describe the freeway landscapes of the United States, which are the opposite of the old "all roads lead to

Rome" centripetal systems of the first world. Then there are the gridded landscapes of the Mississippi territories, which arise out of a classical sense of order that is fitting to the times they were made: they are contemporary with Regency Brighton.

"That reminds me," says Gareth, "You know the expulsion of the Native Americans in the unorganized territories went on at the same time as the Civil War in the east? The Indian wars of the eighteen sixties? The settlers wiped out the buffalo to starve the Indians out."

It's guns and the landscape again. Suddenly I have had enough of Gareth's naive high-explosive landscaping techniques. I get ossified. I sit him down and read him Wilfred Owen's poem "Exposure." It is a poem of despair, about being in the trenches on the Western Front in the winter, watching dawn rising in the east over the enemy trenches, the sleet coming on like a German ally, and finding that the moist eyes of the men who died the day before have turned to ice overnight. Gareth yawns his young man's yawn and stretches his arms, so his *Fuck You All* T-shirt rides up over his belly. His smooth flesh snaps straight back into repose without a hitch. He has not felt a word—it's the same callousness that makes him good for cannon fodder.

The next day he brings me the John Jackson book I lent him, open at the page where the great man applauds the military view of the landscape: the way that soldiers fighting a battle are in intimate harmony with every hedge and hillock, and with every road and river and every source of food and shelter and cover; the way that generals play the landscape like an instrument. He cannot wipe the beam off his face.

"Okay, Gareth," I give in, "you're hired. We are going to the Somme to photograph the battlefields. You carry the camera and the maps and the bread bin; I'll drive."

We slipped into France under cover of the tunnel that runs from Folkestone to Calais and went hurtling off down the A26 toward Arras, with the broad horizons of Artois opening up before us, like a computer screen scrolling. The summer was blazing, and Gareth sat with his window wide open and the slipstream tugging his immaculate forelock—we were both still feeling the islander's opening perception of the Continent, a sudden realization of hugeness that makes you feel you could carry on all the way to Vladivostok. It's like being rich. We stopped at a service station full of Coca-Cola umbrellas and yellow concrete sun shades. Gareth was still carrying the John Jackson book, and he described a circuit of coincidence he had discovered that starts with the Great White Hope of 1910. This was the nickname of a caucasian boxer who was put forward as a challenger to the invincible black heavyweight of the time, Jack Johnson. Now *Jack Johnson* is what American troops in the St. Mihiel sector of the Western Front in 1917 called the big German howitzers, whose shells went up in a cloud of black smoke. Do I get it? he wanted to know. Well, sure—Jack Jackson is a spoonerism for John Jackson. I told him that polar exploration was a feature of the prewar years, and that *Great White Hope* could be a pun on *Great White Way,* which was a popular book at the time, about Antarctica. When Shackleton escaped from his stranded expedition and reached South Georgia in the middle of 1916, he was surprised to find they were still fighting the war in Europe. Everyone had thought it would be over inside three months.

"Did time fly in the trenches, too?" asked Gareth. "I'm twenty-one in three months' time." He looked at me, almost—but not quite—appealing for some wisdom. "I don't feel twenty-one."

So we talked about how sometimes time seems to go slower, sometimes faster. He told me about technology and war—how war distorts time and accelerates technological development, and catches out old generals, who continue to fight the war they learned as captains. I told him about a trick I've learned for getting through the winter. The longest night comes on December 22—so, two full days before Christmas, even, you can say, the days are getting longer, spring is on its way. You can endure January with equanimity.

"Too bad it works the other way around," said Gareth, not getting the point. "The summer starts leaking away right after the twenty-first of June!"

"But what's to endure, in July and August?" I explained to him.

We climbed back in the car and went through the tollbooth and off into the secondary road system toward the valley of the Somme. Down dead straight roads, past green wheat fields, yellow rape fields, hay fields rashed with bright red poppies—*blood soaked,* insisted Gareth, *like the fields of Shiloh*—and fields full of blue flax. Flax flowers look wonderfully opaque, like blue oil paint. We were making for the Ancre valley, the scene of General Douglas Haig's great offensive—the Somme offensive—of July 1916. It was the one that claimed the most casualties, more even than the concentrated killing at Verdun, which is another hundred miles away down the line. It is straightforward to blame Haig and his generals for casually breaking their armies on the stone of the German defenses, but in fact their preparations were minute and painstaking; the weakness was in not adapting when those arrangements went wrong—and, cavalry men that they all were, in that they took so long to wake up to the value of the tank.

We threaded through the back roads of Picardy toward the Somme, taking in Azincourt along the way. On the main street, and in the gas station, there are cut-out figures of archers in chain mail, painted in lurid colors, and a little battlefield museum. Theme-parking of the most basic kind. Then on to Beauquesne, Haig's headquarters during the offensive, where everything was as quiet as bed linen. There were dogs sleeping on their backs in the middle of auto-free streets. There was a boule pitch set among the pleached lime-trees of the village square. Beauquesne is as it has been for centuries, with old slates and old lead and old stone-plinthed buildings with cobbled courts behind them. The roofs have delicate splays at the eaves, and cast-lead ball-and-obelisk finials at the hips. The stone church had buttresses on each corner of the tower, with huge decorative value added: Gareth called it D'Artignan's France. The point of stopping there was that the place is twelve miles behind the 1916 trench lines, and so it is a village unspoiled by bombardment. Later in the day, we traveled to the villages on the line—Beaumont-Hamel, Serre, and Puisieux—to see the difference. These are the places that were reduced to dust in the conflict and rebuilt in the 1920s. The new work, seventy years old now—as old as an old man—is a sort of poor brick vernacular, special to the Western Front, full of an end-of-architecture fuss of dentils and stringcourses, as complicated as straps on a corset, with roofs made of sad red concrete pantiles. The churches, rebuilt in brick, wear bits of plain stone decoration on corbelled brackets. At Puisieux the children in the street shouted at us and our strange revolving panoramic camera, and Gareth said they were calling for help. They looked as though they were planning to escape as soon as they were old enough to ride a moped.

However—outside the villages, past their little town cemeteries with their gray granite memorials peeping over the hedges like cattle, past the statues of soldiers and angels waving wreaths, you come out onto a big, beautiful, gently undulating arable landscape. Perfect for a tank battle. Perfect for defending a trench against an infantry attack, because they have to cross this open landscape in full view of your machine guns. Disastrous, however, for attacking that same trench line in the way they were ordered to back in 1916.

From the road, the little field cemeteries sit in the distance like formal paradise gardens. There is a glimpse of lawn behind a hedge or a wall: a row of white headstones kissed with roses, a tall white cross just high enough to crest the undulations of the land. Every so often there is a bigger cemetery, as at Pozières with a thousand graves in it, a big wall around, and a gate house and pavilions.

The fields are dotted with copses, like the fox-hunting country of central England, although here the copses are for supplying wood rather than fox-earths—and the cemeteries fit into the field-and-copse pattern as though they have always been there. The ordinary order of agricultural practice dominates the scene, from the track of the spraying machines traversing the fields to the cultivated stems of wheat and maize and peas all maturing at a similar height, all planted in rows. The horticulture of the cemeteries is a jump in scale and precision. The grass inside is kept mowed at level zero, the edges of the lawns are cut with a knife, the beech hedges are shorn like soldier's haircuts, and the flowers are immaculately dead-headed.

Along the twenty-mile British front of the Somme offensive, from Gommecourt to Montauban, these cemeteries are so frequent that the next two are usually visible from the one you're in, like the villages. They lie spaced along the old German trench line at six-hundred-yard intervals, perhaps two hundred graves in each one, and each one is given the soldier's name for where they are. *Serre Road 3, Railway Hollow,* and *Luke Copse* are in the ridge above Serre Village, and they have in them the graves of men who died in the first hours of the Somme offensive, on 1 July 1916, when their attack on the German front line was annihilated. Eight hundred yards further into what was enemy territory is another string of four lying along the German support line, which was called *Munich Trench.* Here are the graves of the last men who died, five months later. If you look up from this point, you can see, three miles away, the huge memorial to the missing at Thiepval. It is the most grand of all the battlefield memorials, not completed until 1932, and it has all the heft and height of a cathedral. It does the same job, too, glowering over the country for miles around. It stands on top of what was the German stronghold at the center of the Somme offensive front, the Schwaben redoubt—and the seventy thousand names carved into it are the names of British and Empire soldiers whose bodies could not be found after the war. The field cemeteries have actual skeletons in them, packed side by side, a layer of bones six feet down, each skeleton with its own dog tag, each under its own headstone. At the Thiepval Arch are remembered the names of those who could not be buried—those whose bodies had disintegrated in the shell fire.

The mauve summer haze obscured the five-mile horizon as Gareth and I walked, soaked in sweat, along the line of cemeteries all the way from Beaumont-Hamel to Serre. We crossed paths again and again with a couple, a man and a woman, who seemed to be doing the same thing. She had a camcorder attached to her eyesocket and was chatting to her future audience like someone talking to herself. Later in the day, at Peake Wood Cemetery above Contalmaison, we came across her staging their arrival by filming her spouse as he drove up in their little white Peugeot Cabriolet. What were they playing at? I wanted to shake them and tell them to imagine lines of soldiers lying on the ground with their chests ripped open by shrapnel, screaming for help, but Gareth stopped me. He reminded me that this is a theme park, not a church. It's a place you take your own stories to, not a place where you follow the rules.

In the distance the tower of the Thiepval Arch was as pink as livers in the hazy sun. It may look like a cathedral, but it's not one. It has no interior: I think of it more as a landscape than as a building.

All around us in the fields was the smell of chamomile, so sweet it's sickly. The heat of the day was pulling sausage-sized crane flies out of the grass in swarms, and half a dozen skylarks were singing hard for possession of the merciless sky. Underneath that arch was plenty of cool shade waiting, brimming with as much calm and succor as one of the smooth-surfaced lakes on the river Somme itself. We felt pulled toward it.

Three big tourist buses are filling the parking lot with white painted metal and tinted glass. They are ticking loudly, cooling down after the long haul from the coast. The great arch itself is set on a lawn, among trees, and picnic parties from the buses are spread out in circles wherever there is shade. The tower that you can see from a distance is brought to ground on sixteen huge piers, faced in stone, each with nearly five thousand names carved on it. Every name is in serifed roman letters; every letter has red lead stroked into it by hand. The stones have wreathes carved in them, with the names of the hard-fought pieces of ground where all these men's bodies disappeared. At the center, on a plinth, which you reach by generous, shallow steps, is the cenotaph stone. Twelve feet long, it has a subtle entasis curving across its laterals, fractions of circles whose center is nine hundred feet below the surface of the ground; and another converging its perpendiculars to a point one thousand feet above.

"Does it mean heaven and hell?" asks Gareth, bending down to squint along the curving lines.

"It's a meditation," I say. "The men who designed this thing had India in their bones."

There are stones like this in all the larger cemeteries. Here at Thiepval the stone is the centerpiece of an intended meditation on the once deadly, now recovered, landscape that is spread out below you, and every day it is freshly garlanded with personal tributes to a few of those whose names are up there on the walls. One of today's is a compact disc, of all things, wrapped up in paper poppies, of music by a promising composer cut off before his time.

Suddenly, behind us on the steps, there is a disturbance.

"That's not the whole story," says a tremulous old man, his voice petulantly soaring. "If you're going to tell that, get it right!" The sound of his complaint ricochets up the arch, twanging as it goes. He sounds like a jackdaw. Looks like one, too—one of those skinny old things with sharp white hair and clothes hanging loosely off him. He turns around to the innocently bystanding Gareth and says to him, "Of course we should've used tanks before we did! We should've had combined operations. We should've had radios to stay in touch with each other. All those things could have been there, but no one gave them to us!" Gareth, nodding furiously, understands his *new technology for a new war* position perfectly.

"Can you dig, lad?" asks the old man, starting to prod him in the chest. "Can you dig? Taught me to dig, those buggers did! My spade was more use to me than my rifle!"

He is hopping mad with his tour guide for "getting it all wrong" and calls it the "straw that broke the camel's back" and strides off to extract his luggage from the bus, much to everyone's amusement. Gareth hurries after him and offers to carry the bag. He recognizes a kindred spirit.

"That's right, lad! I earned my respect! And I don't mean to stand around and have it pilfered by buggers like him!" and he jerks a thumb in the direction of his tour party, all hooting with laughter at his antics.

"Mind how you go, Bill," they shout, "burst a bloody blood vessel if you're not careful!"

Another bus has pulled up. A party of Canadians gets out, all wearing Panama hats and sweating like pigs. Their air conditioning has broken down. They pass by the panting, furious Bill and his young helper, thinking that the Thiepval Arch is more like an embarkation camp than a place of meditation. Bill is adamant about not rejoining the tour. He ostentatiously plants his suitcase in the shadow of the big arch and plants himself on it, with his back to the parking lot. He smiles at Gareth.

"When you're my age, lad, you can do what you want."

"How old are you?" asks Gareth, falling for it.

"I'm as old as the century, I am. What year is it? That's how old I am. What year was it when I was loading shells into the back of an eighteen pounder five kilos from here? Nineteen sixteen? I was sixteen then, wasn't I?"

Gareth asks him how he remembers something that happened so long ago.

"Ever seen your best friend sliced in two by a piece of hot metal? Thought not! You won't forget that!"

"Did you know what you were fighting for, if you were only sixteen?" I asked him.

"I joined up for fun! I was fighting for fun!" He stood up and punched the air, his fist zipping past my cheek. "Always enjoyed a bit of a punch up!"

"From what I've heard, it was no fun at all," I said.

"No sir, it wasn't," he said, rearranging himself on his suitcase. "It wasn't till I got home that I realized what it was about. The European Civil War, is what it was."

"Germany fighting France and Britain is a civil war?"

"If Europe is a federation it is," piped up Gareth. Bill held up his bony hand, all covered in little brown spots of tan, and ticked his explanation off on his fingers.

"One: Germans try and take over the whole of Europe, thinking to make it into Greater Germany. Two: we stop them. Three: Hitler tries it again. Four: we stop them. Five: we organize a trade entity."

"A trade entity?" queries Gareth.

"You turning into a parrot, lad?" says Bill. He holds up his other hand and sticks up his thumb. "Step six is a proper federation: United States of Europe, not nations, mind you, states, House of Representatives, Senators, Bill of Rights, the whole works." He jabs a finger at me: "That's your generation's job. I don't know why you don't get on with it, you buggers."

Gareth is still mystified. "What about the Americans? They fought those wars, too."

"And your generation's job is to shut up and do what you're told. That's what I did. Kill Germans, they told me, so that's what I did."

People Bill's age who are still as vigorous as he is are obviously in possession of lucky magic, so even when they say, *Shut up and do what you're told,* you do it. We sit quietly while he lights a cigarette. He looks as if he's going to say, *Drink moderate, smoke moderate, fuck moderate, live to be a hundred!* but Gareth gets in first.

"Do you still dream about it, then?"

"I dream about the mud and bullets. I lie in bed sometimes wide awake and dream about it, if it's a dark night. When I got home and my brother showed me the mark on his shin he got from stumbling about in the bloody blackout the day the bloody Zeppelin came, I knocked him downstairs. Bloody did, the bugger! What does he know about a dark night? What does he know about mud and bullets!"

"What was worse, the boredom or the fear?"

"What boredom, lad?"

"From sitting in the trenches, waiting."

"What was I waiting for?"

"I meant," said Gareth, faltering, "it was such a static war, a stalemate—" the explanation trails off.

"Static!" says Bill, grinning widely. "Fourteen hundred miles an hour not quick enough for you, lad? Speed of a bullet not fast enough for you?" He laughed and slapped his scrawny thigh and pulled on his cigarette and winked at me.

The rest of Bills' party had climbed back on board the bus, fired the engine up, waited a few seconds, and then slowly pulled off. They left him behind.

"They're teasing you," I said. "They'll go around the wood and be back for you in five minutes"—but they weren't. An hour later we were still sitting there, and Bill, who had probably had this coming to him since they left Calais, the cantankerous old sod, was still with us.

"Well then," said Gareth, looking at me with his eyebrows raised. "We're off to Ypres and the Messines Ridge. Want to come with us?"

"Can't stay here," said Bill, and shoved out his hand for us to shake. "William Edwards, Royal Horse Artillery and citizen of Europe, at your service."

—————————— PARKSCAPE ——————————

When you travel the line of the Western Front, you will find cemeteries strung all the way along it. There are French, German, and American cemeteries as well as the British empire ones I've been describing. Every French village has its statue of a soldier, bearing words of gratitude, and although there are many French military cemeteries, they have concentrated their memorial effort around Verdun, where there is a huge ossuary—a collection of bones. Also at Verdun is the *Trance des bayonets*. Part of the French trench line collapsed, burying men in it as they stood there, bayonets fixed. The bayonets sticking out of the ground were the only evidence of what had happened. The entire intact phenomenon is protected by a concrete roof—although no one knows how long the bayonets will survive the souvenir hunters. The few American cemeteries are grand, spacious axial gardens with fountains and towers. The German ones are large empty lawns, subdued and melancholic, with rows of short gray granite crosses.

There are four other concentrations of memorials besides the Somme and Verdun. There is the industrial land of Artois, threaded with railways and superhighways and big, smoking towns. There are the magnificent heights of the Aisne, where a statue of Napoleon looks out over a horizon so

Commonwealth War Graves Commission cemetery near Wulvergem, on the Messines Ridge, Belgium. Photograph by the author.

huge it disappears over the edge of the world. This is where he fought his last stands against the Germans—allied to the British at that time—in 1813. There is the straggling, congested Flanders plain between Béthune and Armentières, and there is the area around the city of Ypres, in Belgium. At the memorial in Ypres, the Menin Gate, the last post is still sounded by buglers in memory of the missing every single evening of the year at eight o'clock. Look at your watch: how long is it to eight in the evening, Belgian time? This is the high point of the active workings of the Western Front theme park, a piece of real theater, with real emotion and real purpose. It is matched by the patient maintenance of the gardeners out there in the field cemeteries. Ypres is another rebuilt place, a medieval city re-created from scratch since 1919. All the buildings, all the houses, the squares, the cathedral, and the city walls have been rebuilt from a base of rubble. The great Flemish Cloth Hall with its loggia and its huge roof was not completed until 1962. It seems real, too, but there is the very faintest shadow of replica about it. It would take a doctorate to chronicle just how and why—perhaps they have been too thorough.

Ypres is our destination now. In answer to Gareth's probing, Bill has finally cleared up the matter of Americans in the European Civil War.

"The Yanks were our friends," he says, and leaves it at that.

"And the Japanese in War Two?" says Gareth. "Was that part of the Civil War as well?"

Bill looks at him, stony faced. "Like I said, the Yanks were our friends." With that, he turned his shriveled brown face toward the roof of the car and went to sleep.

The huge numbers of graves we've seen are having their effect. I remember rushing past the Marathon Mound in Greece once, when the people I was with could not be persuaded to stop. *Gotta catch the ferry!* they snarled. The Marathon Mound is a simple mound of earth in which are interred the Athenians who died defending Greece against the Persian invasion twenty-five hundred years ago. If they had not succeeded, there would have been no Periclean Athens, so people hold up the battle as a pivot in Western history. My point is that in this mound lie buried just 192 men—whereas in the first day of the Somme offensive the British lost twenty thousand. *Oh, twentieth century!* I thought, with tears rolling—one emotional human in a world of six billion—*'Tis of thee!*

The road across the Flanders plain through Armentières dribbles along through a continuous mess of little houses, shops, and market gardens. The density of settlement, after the wide open horizon of the Somme, feels like having fleas. Somewhere along the road the border between France and Belgium passes without remark. It's a pity Bill the federalist is asleep. The cemeteries are still there, still as close together, but here they are shoehorned into empty plots in the ribbon of buildings that line the road, all mixed in with daily life. When at last the ribbon development stops and we ascend the hill onto the Messines Ridge, which lies immediately south of Ypres, Bill wakes up. Gareth has had his head buried in the *Official History of the War,* which is full of detailed maps showing the battlefields down to yards of difference, and which discusses progress of the operations down to the minute, so he can tell us all about the battle fought out here. The taking of the Messines Ridge was a little success sandwiched between the inconclusive horrors of the Somme and the third battle of Ypres, otherwise known as Paschendaele. The German front line ran across the top of the ridge, and so the British—Welsh, in this case—dug nineteen mines into the side of the hill and packed them full of high explosive directly under the German line.

"It was like a bombardment and a surprise attack combined," explained Gareth. The two-week-long bombardments that preceded most offensives had become nothing so much as advertisements that an attack was about to take place. At Messines, the bombardment and the surprise were combined in one almighty explosion that destroyed the German front line at a stroke.

"They heard the explosion a hundred and seventy miles away, in Whitehall," said Gareth. "The sound must have taken a few minutes to get there." I imagined army staff standing in Horse Guards parade with stopwatches, ear trumpets at the ready. I told Gareth about seeing a band practice on Horse Guards one night, a marching battalion of grenadiers, all in busbies.

"They were two hundred yards away at the most. It was easy to see what you could to to them with a couple of Maxim guns."

"You buggers think it's all soldiers and shooting," pipes up Bill from the back seat. Refreshed by his snooze but with previous conversation obliterated, he says, "You want me to tell you what fourteen eighteen was? It was the great European Civil War, that's what!"

We stopped and got out to look at one of the craters. They are still there, full of water, making circular lakes about eighty yards across. Messines is cow country, and in the field stood a Charolais bull looking like Mr. Universe. They have great muscle tone, Charolais, and very short hair.

"He looks just like you, young feller!" said Bill, and it struck me, as we all chortled together, how good it was to have three ages together, old, middle, and young, to see this landscape of memory. Then it was on to Ypres, through the Menin Gate, to settle down in a café in the Great Square with Belgian beer to drink, and one last subject to cover before the buglers played.

———

If I die, think only this of me, that there's a corner of a foreign field that is forever England. It took us two hours to thrash through the topic, and I still ended up dissatisfied. The poem is part of Rupert Brooke's quintet of sonnets *1914,* written early enough in the war for the idea of a "noble sacrifice" to have been tenable. The gist is that the dust of his bones is a special dust, compounded of the physics of England, *a body of England's, breathing English air, washed by the rivers, blest by suns of home.*

"But would that not be the sun that rises in the east and sets in the west, as it does in every other place on earth?" was my question. After two years of the war the superficiality of nationhood had become apparent, at least on the battlefield, where the similarity of all human bodies, rotting down into the soil, and the similarity of the soil itself all over the face of the earth, denies the differences over which wars are fought.

"What makes a corpse like a field is not what makes England different from France," was how we left it, although we had seen for ourselves that the British Army *has* taken corners of foreign fields and *is* maintaining them as pieces of territory possessed by its dead. It is eighty years later, now, and still the British clip and mow and prune as assiduously as if the cemeteries were the palace gardens themselves. They say the maintenance of the cemeteries will go on forever— and if you have ever wondered how it is possible to commemorate the dead without glorifying the war, they have discovered it. They insist on specificity. *This body in this place now,* they say, adding a touch of hope: *and forevermore.* It's the generalities that glorify a war, and the British Army does that too, with its flags and its regimental traditions—but it does it elsewhere.

The idea for the war cemeteries did not come from the army. Men killed were as far as possible buried in some corner of the battlefield, in graves marked by wooden crosses, as the dead of the Crimea or The Peninsular campaign had been. It was a job for soldiers to do, for they would hope that someone would do the same for them—on Vimy Ridge in 1917 the Canadian division organized themselves to dig their own mass burial pit before they started the assault. There was a Red Cross volunteer, called Fabian Ware, who had traveled to France with a makeshift unit in the first months of the war to help the wounded however he could. He noticed straightaway how haphazard these field burials were. Clusters of bodies were buried together, sometimes a hundred in a pit with a lone wooden marker, sometimes a few together where a shell had hit. There were solitary graves in isolated fields where someone had been killed by a sniper. There were empty graves, too, where the upper classes had managed to retrieve their sons for burial back in England. As he worked up and down the front, Ware recorded these graves and the names on them whenever he could. He met mothers who had crossed the Channel and ventured into the war zone desperately seeking the remains of their lost boys. He talked to priests who pointed hopelessly at village cemeteries overflowing with new graves. He realized that he could get a grip on the problem, and he sold his idea to the British high command on the practical grounds that the prospect of burial in a well-marked grave would help the morale of the men.

As he organized his forces to start the great collection of names and bodies, he stumbled across an even greater idea. How could it be justified that the rich could afford to repatriate their sons' remains when the poor could not? That the rich boys would lie in churchyards under marked stones and the poor boys vanish into the mud, when they had all suffered this thing together? He conceived of a great uniformity of burial, one stone for every man, all of them buried near where they had fallen, all ranks and all religions together. It was just one of the twentieth century's experiments in concentrated equality, but it was one that had benevolence at its base. Back home, the voices of the establishment were furious. Class, race, and religion all struggled to maintain the differences Ware's clean plan was proposing to iron out. Reason prevailed; no doubt the fear of what would happen to public opinion if hundreds of thousands of dead soldiers started to fill English village cemeteries played its part.

Ware stayed with the project all his life and became marinated by the poetic grandeur of it. He gave biblical names to the simple concepts that framed it. On *Armistice Day*, on the eleventh hour of the eleventh day of the eleventh month every year, the *Million Dead* were commemorated by the *Great Silence.* He called the thousand cemeteries, and the four vast memorials that listed the names of the missing, *These Cities of the Dead.* He believed that their presence in the world would exert such a terrible hold on the memory that they would make another war impossible.

At twenty hundred hours, we gather with two hundred other people at the Menin Gate to listen to the Last Post. The long, slow notes of the bugles fill our hearts. At the end, all the tourists clap and disperse, except for Bill, who stands still for two whole minutes, reenacting something that only his generation really understands, the *Great Silence.* It is a sort of secular prayer, in which no words are spoken. If you wanted to study a sacred landscape, I think you would go to Jerusalem, home of the Temple and the Wailing Wall and the Holy Sepulchre and the Dome of the Rock: full of the sounds of prayer and the clash of beliefs. Watching Bill, standing stiff as a standard, I realized that the Western Front landscape has achieved something I would not have thought possible—a secular sacred landscape. Now, when people shudder and say to me, "Oh, Picardy, it's so grim there, with all those gravestones," I disabuse them.

"You silly buggers!" I say, "it's beautiful!"

EPILOGUE

The wilderness is not just something you look at; it's something you are part of. You live inside a body made of wilderness material. I think that the intimacy of this arrangement is the origin of beauty. The wilderness is beautiful because you are part of it.

Cultivation—the work of humans—has a different sort of beauty. There is nothing else under the sun than what there has always been. Cultivation is the human reordering of the material of the wilderness. If it is successful, the beauty of it lies in the warmth of your empathy for another human's effort.

Landscape is a huge subject, as big as the earth and its atmosphere and reaching out to the edge of the universe. The big moves in landscape happen very rarely. You will be lucky to see one during your lifetime and even luckier to be in the right place at the right time to be involved in the making of it. Incremental changes happen all the time, however. They gradually accrue to big changes in what there is in the world, and whatever you are up to, you will be involved in these already. My epilogue is: be aware of the strategy that governs what you do.

The White Horse turf-cut figure on White Horse Hill, Oxford, England. Photograph by the author.